IT CUTS ME DEEPLY
A JOURNEY THROUGH MY LIFE

RICHARD BURTON

authorHOUSE

AuthorHouse™ UK
1663 Liberty Drive
Bloomington, IN 47403 USA
www.authorhouse.co.uk
Phone: 0800 047 8203 (Domestic TFN)
 +44 1908 723714 (International)

© 2020 Richard Burton. All rights reserved.

No part of this book may be reproduced, stored in a retrieval system, or transmitted by any means without the written permission of the author.

Published by AuthorHouse 05/11/2020

ISBN: 978-1-7283-5294-7 (sc)
ISBN: 978-1-7283-5293-0 (e)

Print information available on the last page.

Any people depicted in stock imagery provided by Getty Images are models, and such images are being used for illustrative purposes only.
Certain stock imagery © Getty Images.

This book is printed on acid-free paper.

Because of the dynamic nature of the Internet, any web addresses or links contained in this book may have changed since publication and may no longer be valid. The views expressed in this work are solely those of the author and do not necessarily reflect the views of the publisher, and the publisher hereby disclaims any responsibility for them.

I dedicate this book to
my sons Kenny, Alex, and Andrew;
my daughter-in-law, Sam;
my grandchildren Cayden and Hope;
my sisters Annette and Josephine;
my brothers Thomas and James;
my ex-partner, Liz;
all my nieces and nephews, of which there are too many to name; and
in memory of Jim Houston and Michael Patterson, killed in action.

People will do anything no matter how absurd in order to avoid facing their own soul.

Carl Jung

"The Life That I Have"
The life that I have
Is all that I have
And the life that I have
Is yours.

The love that I have
Of the life that I have
Is yours and yours and yours.

A sleep I shall have
A rest I shall have
Yet death will be but a pause.

For the peace of my years
In the long green grass
Will be yours and yours and yours.
Poet Leo Marks

"I truly believe every single person has to go through something that absolutely destroys them so they can figure out who they really are."

My name is Richard Burton. I was born on 12 March 1959, at 1.25 on a Thursday morning. Number one in the music charts was the Platters' "Smoke Gets in Your Eyes."

My earliest childhood memories were of growing up in Glasgow. I come from a working-class family with a Catholic background. I'm the oldest of five and have two brothers and two sisters. My dad, Joseph, was a hardworking man, employed in the heavy industries of ship building and steelworks. My mother, Elsie, was a housewife.

The streets of Glasgow were tormented by razor gangs and money lenders at almost every corner and in every pub. Poverty was rife and the housing was Dickensian, with outside toilets and no hot running water. We used a tin bath in front of the fire on a Sunday evening, starting with the oldest and coming down to the youngest, so by the time the last one got in, the water was black. Hence the saying "Don't throw the baby out with the bathwater". Monday to Saturday it was a quick wash at the sink: face, neck, and crotch.

We initially lived in a council house with hot running water and an inside toilet. My dad had lived there since 1931. The house had been passed down to him from his parents.

Dad married Mother in 1958 and then moved into that same house, where I lived after I was born and then my brothers Thomas and James, shortly followed by my sister Annette. Life was good at this time for the family, and it was a loving household.

At that time Dad worked in the railway parcel section, loading the trains heading for London, and he brought back loads of expensive clothing and meat that the railway men would "forget" to load onto the train. He gave my mother a red sequined velvet dress, and she wore it on

New Year's Eve. She looked beautiful. Every time I look at my niece, I can see my mother. This was 1963, and my dad had actually loaded the train (Glasgow to London mail train) that was robbed by The Great Train Robbers that year.

I started school in the summer of 1964 and attended the same one my dad had gone to. On my first day I was scared, and he carried me on his shoulders, with my school uniform on – short trousers and little cap – and school bag on my back. I had a nun as a teacher, with her long habit and veil with the white fringe around the head and long rosary beads hanging from her waist. She hit you with the blackboard duster if you didn't pay attention.

At the age of 5, sitting in a class among thirty pupils, I felt nothing but fear. We went out to the playground at breaktime, and I, being very small, was pushed over by the bigger boys all running about. I tumbled and ended up with a massive lump on my forehead. That was why I hated my first day of school and continued to hate it until I left at 16.

My siblings and I were all lying in bed on a particular Sunday evening. Looking up at the ceiling, I could see up in the loft was drilling through with a pencil. Dad came into the room and told us to be quiet.

He went next door to the neighbour and told him that some guys were up in the loft. The coal bunker was on the landing, and my dad jumped up and tried to get the loft door opened. But they must have been sitting on it.

Dad said to him, "You stay here, and I'll go down the backcourt and see if I can see them on the roof".

He looked up and saw them coming out of the skylight, so Dad climbed the drainpipe and chased them all across the roofs, but he never caught them.

We got invited to a birthday party of a friend that lived in our street. We sat down to jelly, ice cream, and fruit and it was great – until their dad turned up drunk.

As soon as he saw us there, he said, "Why are they in my house?" and threw us out.

My mother went crazy and told my dad when he came home from work. He went straight up to the guy's house and they had a fight. Two days later the same guy put an axe through his wife's head. She crawled across the road toward her sister's but never made it. She died on the road.

One day my little pal and I are looking in a shop window, and this old guy came up to us and asked if we would like a bar of chocolate. We looked at each other and said yes, and he said, "Come up this close first."

We followed him to the next landing, and he took out his penis and started to masturbate. We didn't really understand what he was doing. He gave us money to go into the shop to buy chocolate.

I got home and stood by the fire eating my Fry's Cream bar, and my mother asked me where I got it from. I told her, and we went to my friend's mum's house to tell her, and then off to the police station we went. We gave a description of this old man, but nothing ever came of it. All this so far, and I was only 5 years old.

My auntie Annie came back from America. She'd been working as a nanny for some bigshot lawyer in New York, and he was friends with the Hollywood actor Vincent Price. Annie said he was at their dinner parties quite frequently, but she didn't like it and wanted back home. She brought us cowboy shirts and cowboy hats, and this was the real thing. We all thought we were Roy Rogers.

About late 1964 my mother suffered a relapse of tuberculosis. My two brothers contracted it too, and my sister was born with a hole in her heart, and all of them were in hospital for a very long time – I don't mean months; it was about a year, maybe longer. It was a very difficult time for my dad. His wife was dying and possibly three of his children. I was packed off to Auntie Josephine's, my mother's older sister. She was very good to me and showed me a lot of love. They had a good standard of living, at least compared to us. They had a car and a telephone and took me on trips to Stirling in their caravan.

But all I wanted was to be with my dad and mother along with my brothers and sister, but it wasn't to be, at least not for now. I visited them in hospital, but they were in three different locations between Glasgow and East Kilbride.

My mother was lying on her back in an iron lung and could only see me through a mirror above her head, and then on to another hospital I went to see my brothers, Thomas and James, looking at them in a cot. Thomas wore callipers so that his legs would get strong enough to support his body weight and in time hopefully would be able to walk again. James was the same, but he didn't have to wear those terrible things, as he was younger and wasn't quite old enough to stand yet. They had contracted TB and meningitis of the brain and spine and were very lucky to have survived.

And then it was off to another hospital to see my sister Annette, who had a hole in the heart. She was so tiny and had all sorts of tubes coming out of her. We weren't allowed to touch her.

On Easter Sunday 1965, I was taken by my auntie Josephine and uncle Craig, along with my cousin, to see my dad and to get my Easter egg. My cousin sat beside me in Uncle Craig's brand-new Ford Corsair. She had a large, plain, chocolate Easter egg in a basket with a big bow on it.

I walked into my house. Dad was mopping the floor. We only had linoleum as we couldn't afford carpets. I can still smell the disinfectant to this day. I could see the look of sorrow on Dad's face. Almost all his family was in hospital, and he worked twelve-hour shifts in the steelworks and sat alone at night.

He gave me my Easter egg, a little sixpenny one, as that was all he could afford. We didn't stay long as Auntie Josephine had other business to attend to. I got back in the car and burst out crying. I longed to stay with my dad. My cousin offered me a piece of her egg, and I said no. To this day I don't eat plain chocolate.

I continued to get passed around between my granny and uncle and back to Auntie Josephine. I couldn't stay at my dad's as he had to work to keep a roof over our heads. There was no housing benefit in those days. If you didn't pay your rent, you were out of the house.

Because of that early experience, I have never felt like I belonged or that I was ever good enough. It left an emptiness in me. Maybe the psychology of it had something to do with the song that was in the Scottish charts at the time, "Nobody's Child", sung by the Alexander Brothers.

Eventually they all started to come home. I'm not sure who came home first or in what order. I can only assume my mother did, as my dad wouldn't have been able to take care of us. I was thrilled to be back home with all of us together again; it didn't matter to me about going to Stirling in my auntie Josephine's caravan or their comfortable lifestyle; we were together, and that was all that mattered. My mother seemed to go into deep depressions, and when she had been drinking, she took it out on my dad.

On Christmas Eve 1965, my parents were arguing, and Mother hit him on the head with a silver candlestick. At work a couple of days later, Dad was working with lime, and some of it got into the cut on his head. He collapsed and was taken to hospital. The police got involved and wanted to arrest my mother, but he was having none of it. It was my first taste of the violence that my mother dished out on my dad.

As her depression worsened, Dad had to take more time off work. He lost his job and we lost the house, and eviction was coming, so we did our first "moonlit flit".

The song that was in the charts at the time was The Beatles' "Yesterday", and American troops had just been sent to Vietnam by US president Lyndon B Johnson due to the Gulf of Tonkin incident the year prior.

The place we squatted in was a rundown tenement in the East End of Glasgow. The condition was shocking. It was an abandoned building that was due for demolition. it had no ceiling or windows, and plastic sheeting covered the window frame to stop the rain and wind coming in. Unhygienic to say the least – it was rat-infested. We all lived and slept in one room, on a bed in the recess.

We were playing down the backcourt amongst all the half pulled-down wash shelters, throwing bottles against the wall. Remember, we all wore short trousers in those days. Anyway, my brother, Junior, threw a bottle. It bounced of the wall and hit me in the leg, and I ended up with twelve stitches. In those days they didn't give you anything to numb the body part that was to be stitched. They held me down whilst the doctor sewed my leg. It was terrible.

The place was rat-infested, and my brother James brought up six baby rats in a cardboard box, as he thought they were cute. He gave them to my mother, and she nearly took a heart attack, realising the diseases these things carry.

My auntie Josephine sent my cousin up to our place on this particular

Friday to collect me, so that I could spend the weekend with them. But I felt the hurt for my brothers: Why not them? I could never have treated any of my nieces or nephews differently, if I had any at the time.

I still had the stitches in my leg, and the wound became infected, due to the squalor we were living in. I was at my auntie Molly's, my dad's sister, and she cleaned my leg with Dettol and removed the big scab that had grown over the stitches. It had become so badly infected I could have lost my leg.

We went to a school with the playground on the roof. You could see the whole of Glasgow from it. It was a horrible and frightening school, in the poorest part of Glasgow. The teachers were bastards, and it was the no-hopers that came from the poorest in society that only went to those schools. If it hadn't been the law to attend school, none of us would have been taught anything. We would have been street urchins. Yet just two hundred metres down the road was the school that my cousins attended, one of the best in Glasgow, for the brightest students.

We moved from this rundown flat to yet another single-end, one-room flat. All we had was a cooker, sink, and the recess for a double bed. We all slept in this one bed with Mum. Dad slept on two chairs pulled together. It was the same street that a well-known player for Glasgow Celtic lived in, although we didn't know him. It was a very small street, with one shop, a primary school, and a fire station that looked like something out of the *Trumpton* TV series. We lived there for about six months.

My dad found it more and more difficult to get a job, as in those days, when you applied for work, on the application form it would ask what your religion was. If you said Catholic you didn't get the job, and even if you didn't state your religion, they would know by your surname or what school you had attended. All the factories were owned by Protestants, so Catholics had no chance. The same problem was happening in Northern Ireland. England will never understand what it was like to be a Catholic in Glasgow in those days. We were treated like second-class citizens.

I remember the day I made my first holy communion. I wore a kilt, and all the girls wore little white dresses. We all carried rosary beads and the catechism, presented to us by the holy father, which instructed how to live your life according to the Catholic church.

Next, the Protestants' Orange Order walked past and stopped outside the church and played their music. In between the drumbeats, they shouted, "Fenian bastards!" to insult us Catholics. It lives with me to this day. I hate the Orange Order, a hateful bunch of bigots, and today I don't believe in manmade religion of any kind, including Catholicism.

Even then, as a youngster of only 8, I asked myself why were we living in such conditions. Why were our parents going through all this hardship when they had been through so much already? So had my brothers and sister, and now they were getting treated like second-class citizens because they were Catholic.

Things started to look up. One day Dad was signing on the brew (the dole – unemployment), and the young woman asked if he had ever thought of moving to Corby in Northamptonshire.

She said, "We can guarantee you a job and a house to go with it," and he came back home and put it to my mother.

What had they to lose? Scotland and its Protestant factory owners were treating us like dirt on their shoes. That's why to this day I have no loyalty to the English Crown or the Church of England, its Scottish counterpart the Church of Scotland, and its Presbyterian beliefs all configured around a monarchy and a crown, which has no place in a democracy of the twenty-first century.

The only problem with moving to Corby was that Dad would need to go down for six weeks before us to get settled into his new job and to also give the council time to sort out a house for us. In the meantime, he would send money up for my mother. It was great to see a smile on her face. She could buy us shoes and clothes and put food on the table, even though we were still living in complete and utter squalor. It didn't matter; we were moving to greener pastures and a better life. We went round to all the shops in the Gallowgate, collecting boxes for our move.

The six weeks passed, and a van and a driver was hired as Dad didn't drive. Then came the moment to say goodbye to my granny and aunties. That was hard, but we got through it, with anticipation of a pilgrimage to a better life: to a land of milk and honey, and for the first time in our lives, things were going to be better.

Glasgow was finished. It was a dirty and broken slum, through years of neglect after the post-war of a broken and bankrupt Britain that had been forgotten about by the English establishment.

England was thriving, hence they needed to recruit people from Scotland to help rebuild England and build new housing along with steel foundries and infrastructure. Corby was a thriving new town in England, and it was the Scots that were building it and making money for the English Exchequer.

At the same time, being in Glasgow was like living in Dickensian housing conditions, with a bigoted council that was prejudiced against Catholics, who couldn't get a job and got offered the worst housing available.

CORBY HERE WE COME

We got the last steam train ever to leave Glasgow Central Station in the summer of 1967, as the following year trains changed over to diesel, which were faster, cleaner, and cheaper to run. This was also the year that Glasgow Celtic won the European Cup, the first British club to do so, although I don't really remember it happening, which is such a shame.

It was about an eight-hour journey, and we all fell asleep and missed our stop at Kettering. Not a problem, as it was only two stops off. On arrival at Kettering was a taxi booked and paid for by the council to take us to our new home: a brand-new build with back and front garden and not only one toilet, but two, one upstairs and one downstairs. I couldn't believe it. I thought the council had made a mistake. It was seventh heaven.

Dad had done us proud, and Mum was very brave to have left Scotland at a time where people rarely travelled any more than four or five miles from their neighbourhood.

We got unpacked and settled into our new surroundings. Very soon afterwards my auntie Josephine and uncle Craig moved down too and got a job beside my dad in the steelworks. So Corby became known as little Scotland as half of Glasgow and the West Coast of Scotland had moved down for work. Most seemed to be Catholic, as they couldn't get a job back home. As I've mentioned, most if not all the industries were owned and controlled by Protestants.

I was 9 when we started at our new school, where 50 per cent of the teachers were nuns – at that time, the Roman Church had a stronghold over Catholic schools and indoctrinated their beliefs and desire to control through fear and guilt.

On this particular day we were going swimming with the class, and I had forgotten my swimming kit, so the teacher asked me how far my house was from the school. I told him it was only five minutes up the road when in fact I lived about three miles away. He told me I could go home during lunchtime and get my swimming kit.

I rushed out the school gate with excitement, straight on to the road between parked cars, and all I remember is flying through the air and waking up in hospital. I had been hit by a taxi and suffered severe abdominal injuries and some cuts and bruises. I was in intensive care for about four days and in hospital for about ten. My dad tried to make me laugh all the time, and it was painful because of the injuries to my abdomen.

Lots of goodies arrived at the house for when I came out of hospital, as my teacher had arranged it. All my classmates had put together a package of books, which all seemed to be about the RAF and Royal Navy, along with beautiful stuffed birds and farm animals – and of course plenty of sweets. The teacher who had let me come home was in a terrible state of shock and disbelief of what had happened to me. It could have cost the poor guy his career, but all was well that ended well.

After I recovered and started back at school, we were all playing in the coal shed and someone broke the light bulb. The nun in charge beat us with a cane across our hands. It was cruel and barbaric and I hated those evil bitches. She had us praying to God for what seemed like hours, to ask his forgiveness for what we had done. I told my mother, and she went straight down to that school. What she said to that nun I won't repeat. You see, my mother had had nuns as teachers and also had bad experiences with them.

On 31 October 1968, my youngest sister, Josephine, arrived. I remember the day she came home from the hospital. I was 9 years older than her and wanted to hold her first, but my mother passed her straight to my cousin. I felt left out and discarded, the same as I had felt when my mother, brothers, and sister were in hospital and I couldn't live with my dad. It's funny how certain things stick in your mind and how certain events can shape you into the person you become in your adult life.

It Cuts Me Deeply

They say, "Give me a child until he is 7 and I will show you the man." That sentence is attributed to St Ignatius Loyola and also to Aristotle.

For the greater part, I have found my life a very lonely existence, although no one would ever know that about me. I have become insular and very much a loner, and at times people have told me that I am an eccentric. In hindsight I can see it now. I am not perturbed by this; it's part of who I am, and I can't change that. Maybe it was caused by early childhood experiences, maybe it's genetic.

Anyway, getting back to Corby as 1968 rolled into 1969. The Vietnam War is raging and is all over the news, the Troubles kicked off in Northern Ireland, and on 14 August, the British army were deployed to Londonderry to stop the Protestants burning Catholics out of their homes.

My mother, looking as white as a sheet, was taken out of the house in a wheelchair with her legs straight up in the air. I felt really scared that I wouldn't see her again for many years. She had in fact haemorrhaged and was bleeding to death. She was taken straight into the operating theatre, were she died and was dead for quite a few minutes. By the grace of God (if he exists; I personally have my doubts) my mother was allowed to enter this life yet again.

She had beaten TB, when most of her friends had died from this debilitating illness that had taken the youth of not only Scotland but the whole of the United Kingdom. But its biggest casualties were in Glasgow, where by population density had lost more than London, Liverpool, and Manchester combined. This was caused primarily by poor housing, bad sanitation, and overcrowding.

I get so angry, and as I write, the tears roll down my face. I ask myself, "What price must we pay for being poor? What did my mother and father do so wrong to live in such a diabolical existence that was so Dickensian in nature?" We had to endure so much poverty whilst the people responsible lived in splendour in their big mansion houses in the leafy suburbs of Surrey, the West End of Glasgow, and the metropolis of Edinburgh. The politicians and factory owners worked the men of the shipbuilding industries and forged the steel from the white-hot furnaces twelve hours a day for a pittance of pay, whilst these parasites continued to live off the backs of the poor and downtrodden and still do.

However, at this time we were still living in Corby and it was great.

We had a lovely house with beautiful surroundings, a big field right next to our house, and an old pillbox, a type of concrete dug-in guard post used during the Second World War was in the field. We played soldiers in it.

The toy gun and all the latest rage of the time for young boys was a Johnny Seven machine gun. One of the lads that we played with had one, and we used to all get a shot of it. We never owned one as they were quite expensive and had just hit the British market at the time.

We used to make football pendants and play little competitions with the rest of the boys in and around our streets. It was brilliant. The football heroes of the time, certainly in England, were George Best, Billy Bremner, and Denis Law, and we all imagined that we were professional football players. I had a Manchester United top with number 7 on it, the same number as George Best.

We went apple picking in the orchards in the summertime and made dens in the woods. Dad got free tickets from his work and took us to the fairground. It was a magical time. It was truly a lovely place to live. I have so many fond memories of Corby.

My cousin Jane got married to Mark whilst we were down in Corby. I looked up to him as the big brother that I never had. To think they were only 20 and 21 at the time. It was a lovely wedding, and I have great memories of that day.

It was 1969, I was about 10 years old, and for whatever reason my mother decided to move us back to Glasgow. I think she missed her family too much, especially my granny, but in my mind it was the worst decision she would ever make. It would be the catalyst for the onset of complete poverty and alcoholism.

I came up to Glasgow with my mother and two sisters on the coach about a fortnight before my dad and Thomas and James; they stayed behind to pack up the house. We stayed at my granny's.

We went with Mum and her sister Annie to look at the house we were moving into, and it was a complete shitehole on the East End of Glasgow, yet back to our old stomping grounds of Dickensian housing, with an outside toilet, a backcourt that looked like the aftermath of the Somme in Flanders, one room, and a kitchen with an old cast iron range to heat the house.

My dad and brothers arrived in the back of a lorry on 31 December

1969. The impact was immediate; from that moment on, our childhood was over. I was coming up to my 11th birthday, and our fate was sealed. Poverty and alcoholism were about to reach a whole new level.

My mother's drinking steadily increased, with regular visits from my uncle and aunties. Coming home from school, as you approached the door, you could hear all the voices. I entered the house that was thick with cigarette smoke, and they would all be drunk. All I wanted was to come home and watch *Scooby Doo* and get our dinner; instead, it was out the door with a bag of chips. The surroundings weren't pleasant. We stayed out as long as we could, especially in the summer, but when we returned later that night, the drink had really taken hold of them.

Then the arguments started, and they always resulted in violence. It was a frightening experience, as it would be quite vicious, and a weapon would always be used by my mother or her sisters against my dad and uncles. The next day they all had hangovers and sat in silence, not speaking to each other – until someone said, "Let's get a drink." It was usually my mother who made this suggestion, and so it continued, with the same result. People drink to escape their pain and to remove themselves from the existence of no hope, but once alcohol gets a grip on you, it's all over.

Beginning in 1970, my mother lost her personality, looks, and self-respect. We were now living on skid row and mixing with the deadbeats, degenerates, and a subculture of the razor gangs and winos, the likes of which today's generation couldn't even begin to comprehend.

With alcohol being the primary factor in our misfortune, everything else became secondary: food, electric and gas, clothing – nothing was getting paid, so the electric was first to be cut off and then the gas.

Thomas would turn the electric on again, and we'd get caught, so it was cut off again. Thomas turned it back on again, but this time we would take the fuse out after we had a cup of tea in the morning at around eight and then put it back in at five o'clock, as the electricity board only checked between working hours, so we got away with it for a long time.

Poor sanitation gave us all dysentery and sent Thomas off to hospital for a week. We suffered severe cramps and constant diarrhoea, but with the alcoholism came the inevitability of hunger for maybe one or two days at a time. I drank water to fill my stomach and frequently had dizzy spells caused by low blood sugar and weakness.

I don't have good memories of Christmas, because too often we woke on Christmas day, the most magical time of the year for a child, with not only no Christmas presents but no food. I used to watch from the window and see the other kids out on the street with their new bikes and football strips on.

And I never wondered why, even when I was in the army, I avoided Christmas if I could as it brought back too many powerful memories. Even today I don't like Christmas.

Alcoholism robbed us of the sustenance to keep us alive. I don't blame or resent my mother and father for our poverty, I blame a system that bred poverty in Glasgow, the religious bigotry that led to my dad being unemployable, and the shame on this country that treated Catholics, blacks, and the Irish as second-class citizens. My parents were two of the kindest, most honest, God-fearing people you could ever meet and would have done anything for anyone. We will never know the full extent of the suffering my mother went through in her short 63 years on this planet. All I do know is that she loved all of us in equal measure. Wherever she is now, I hope she has at last found peace, because she didn't have any whilst she was on this earth.

My father was a gentleman, something I will never be; he was kind, gentle, and compassionate, never spoke ill of anyone, and saw the best in everyone. He was a beautiful man with a beautiful soul, and the world is a poorer place without him. We had a terrible life but managed to deal with it with wonderful parents who tried their best in the most horrendous circumstances.

All bets were stacked against them from the day I was born. The house we moved into was filthy and riddled with dampness and cold and was just too old. A cast iron range heated the house. James and I slept in a double bed with Thomas in a single next to us, as he occasionally wet the bed due to a nervous disposition that the TB and meningitis had left him with. My mother and father slept in the next room in a bed in the recess, along with my two sisters Annette and Josephine.

The conditions at the time were not typical of every family, but we didn't let it bother us, or so we thought – as I have already said, we were subjected to many days of hunger and abuse from my mother, and gang fights raged outside almost every other night, more so in the summer. I saw my first stabbing when I was about 12 years old, and many times after that I saw guys getting hit with hammers and axes, their faces slashed wide open with throats cut with razors.

One particularly hot summer evening, this guy had been stabbed multiple times all along his back and down his legs. The café owner came out and gave him a chair to sit on, whilst an ambulance had been called. The pavement was on a slight hill, and I watched his lifeblood flow down that hill.

I didn't realise it at the time, but I do believe that was the start of my PTSD. I was 12, and this was 1971, a year before Bloody Sunday in Northern Ireland, a conflict that I would serve in some capacity fourteen years later. It would add to the trauma I had already witnessed as a young boy.

The house we lived in was due for demolition in the summer of 1973, so everyone was getting rehoused and farmed out to the estates on the fringes of Glasgow. As everyone moved out, we still weren't being rehoused and wondered why. We got no answers from Mum or Dad. We were still going hungry and by now weren't even going to school; we were dogging it (playing truant; I know that *dogging* has a different connotation today). We decided we could make money from all those abandoned houses and collected the scrap metal (copper, brass, and lead). We were like children in a sweat shop. There was no such thing as health and safety in those days, no fences around empty flats that were half torn down, just left like that until the men came back on shift the next day. We stripped it all down to the bones – so much so that they put a night watchman on the site, as the workers were being robbed blind and losing a fortune. This is in the days of a popular police programme on TV called *The Sweeney*, about the Metropolitan Police's Flying Squad, starring John Thaw and Dennis Waterman, when brute force was the order of the day and an answer to everything by the British police.

We got a good kicking from those officers, and we were only 12 or 13 years old, but the money to be made from the scrap metal far outweighed any kicking that was forthcoming from the boys in blue.

The most dangerous part of the building was the roof, a four-story Victorian tenement in pretty bad shape. We climbed out onto the roof and stripped the lead that run down the seam of the building, where the chimney divided the two adjoining flats. It ran all the way down to the gutter, and this was very dangerous – this was also where James came into his own; he was fearless and would sit at the edge of the building with both feet on the gutter. One false move and it would be all over and James would be dead. It still puts the fear into me to this day – James too. Both of us are scared of heights now … and to think I went on to do parachuting!

We continued to strip all the houses, as well as feed us. It was a buzz doing it, even the thrill of the chase from the cops, who very rarely ever caught us. We were like the Dead End Kids from the movie *Angels with Dirty Faces*, starring James Cagney.

At this juncture in our lives, Mother had us at chapel every night, especially during lent, the holy week running up to Easter Sunday. We became altar boys, working with the priest doing Mass. In 1973, there were six weeks of power cuts, so that meant the whole country had their electricity rationed to four hours a day. One hour in the morning before going to school was allowed for breakfast to be cooked for the kids. This didn't apply to us because I don't ever remember getting breakfast. Then it would be turned on again at four to allow tea to be cooked, and then it went off just after the news at 6.30, and that would be it until the next morning. This was in the dead of winter, and as we had been altar boys, we would get candles from our priest. The house was lit up like Blackpool Illuminations.

You see, the miners had gone on strike for more pay and better conditions, and the power stations were run by coal, so no coal, no power. There were no candles in the shops either as everyone was panic-buying them.

A great priest, young and good looking, played the guitar and used to take us away at the weekend on church outings and on an annual holiday. We went to a place called Whithorn in the Scottish Borders, and it was the first time I had seen a cow, except for on TV.

The world was a different place in those days, and Glasgow wasn't really part of the world. As my brother James once said to me, there was the poor and then there was us. Our poorness outstripped everyone else's. I remember Dad being told by our priest that he had arranged for Dad to go to the Salvation Army in Glasgow, as they were going to help us out with Christmas presents. I went with him, and when we arrived, a young

Salvation Army woman answered the door to this big Victorian house. Even when I walk past it today, I can still remember the house. We walked in and very few words were spoken. The bag was sitting in the corner waiting for us to collect, so we picked it up and left.

We had to walk back about four or five miles, but it didn't matter as we had to walk there anyway. We got home and gave the bag to my mother, and the house was ablaze with candles from the chapel and wood was burning in the fire. Woodfires are trendy today, but in those days, if you were burning wood, it meant you couldn't afford coal. I felt my mother was hurt and my dad was dejected in his abject failure of his family, and I could see their pain. I can see people's pain, when a system has let them down, and in today's society, I see people that rip the arse out of the system, and it makes me really angry. But in those days, there wasn't a system in place to help the poor; we had to get through it or die.

We got up on Christmas morning to see what the Salvation Army had given us. There was a couple of board games, like Snakes and Ladders and Monopoly and a couple of action men and dolls for the girls. It breaks my heart to this day that my parents had to endure this. That's why I am not a materialistic person. We would recover, but I felt their profound sadness and pain.

Alcohol took hold even more, especially on my mother, and the abuse my dad had to endure along with the violence was unrelenting and ferocious, resulting in my dad being hospitalised to get stitched up. He seldom ever reacted, only in self-defence. That's why today I will not tolerate any woman bringing me down. It's said that we are a product of our environment.

On this Christmas my uncle was staying with us, him being a boxer and apparently a very good one in his day. He came in from the pub and had bought us two figures of Dracula and Frankenstein. He decided that I and my two brothers would fight each other bare knuckled until the blood poured out of us, and whomever won would get first and second prize of these two figures.

My mother, in her drunken state, allowed this to happen. The power of alcoholism and poverty takes away the morality of normal behaviour, and the abnormal becomes the new normal.

They demolished the houses in our street until they got to our building, and my mother refused to move out. We stayed there with no electric, gas, or running water. We had to go to the night watchman, as they were called in those days, for water. Today they're called security guards. We lived there for another two months before being rehoused in yet another shitehole.

The local gang was called the Shamrock, notorious sectarian, vicious Catholic bastards who would cut you open in the blink of an eye.

Throughout our childhood we played truant and were always being taken in front of the authorities, a children's panel, and our mother would invariably be fined. I can't imagine the stress this must have caused my parents. Everything has a cause and effect: poverty and alcoholism brought about our hunger, and because of this, instead of going to school, we went out to steal lead, copper, and brass to feed ourselves. Schooling became non-existent.

We lived there for two years. It was a run-down shitehole, and we were still going hungry, and although there were no buildings lying derelict for us to get scrap metal from, to help feed us, there was a fruit market just across the road.

This was an opportunity as everyone eats fruit and vegetables, so each day the lorries would come in to load up for delivery to the fruit shops and supermarkets, and at the end of the day's deliveries, whatever was left over and close to its sell-by date would be dumped into a skip. We were right in about it, grabbing potatoes, lettuce, cucumbers, and fruit, gathering it into little boxes. We'd go round the doors selling it for half price, and we made quite a few pounds.

In the summertime we made even more money, with all the salad stuff, and every house wanted flowers in their window too, so we would take all the flowers from the skip.

We went round all the houses selling football cards. You basically picked a team, and whatever the hidden team was, if you picked it, you won the money. Of course no one ever won.

This continued until our family got evicted and re had to do another moonlit flit the night before the sheriff's officers (bailiffs) arrived to publicly shame us and throw our stuff out onto the street.

We moved to – or should I say squatted – in a derelict building right next to Celtic football ground. The whole street was due for demolition,

It Cuts Me Deeply

and only four or five houses had anyone living in them, so it was back to stripping the scrap metal from the derelict houses. By now we had become expert.

The house we moved into had no windows or electric or water, and that was soon rectified. We just went round to the other abandoned houses and took the windows that were still whole. Thomas took care of the electric and water.

There was a family that lived just across from us, I can't remember how many of them there were, was but they all wore balaclava hats and were always hitting themselves on the head. I couldn't understand why they were doing this. It turned out their heads were crawling with lice, and they had seeping sores all over their heads. It was too painful to scratch, poor little bastards, and they were being sexually abused by their father.

A large soft drinks factory was just behind our house, and the factory backed onto the graveyard, so on a Sunday night we climbed up the graveyard wall, raced through the cemetery, and jumped onto the lorries. There was a gang of us, and we formed a human chain to offload the juice, by the crate until the lorry was empty. We then went round the houses to sell it.

There was always a way for us to make money. The building was coming down so we eventually moved, but only about five hundred metres up the road to another shitehole. We continued to play truant and strip the scrap metal, and we even broke into a large, well-known shop in Glasgow. We walked past it on a hot summer night, and someone had left a window open above the door – only a small one – so my brother James was tasked to climb in and open the fire escape at the back of the shop.

In we went, and all the idiots that were with us headed straight for the pic 'n' mix bins, we headed for the stuff that could be sold, like clothes, records, and electrical appliances. In fact, we broke into the manager's car, and when we opened the boot, we discovered that this arsehole had been stealing from the shop too. You couldn't make this shit up.

We then broke into a pub at the corner of our street. All the men from the steelworks drank in this pub, and right next to it was an old cottage-type house. The adjoining wall was really thick, so we decided to dig through the wall in the afternoon whilst all the punters were in the pub drinking.

We had watched *The Great Escape* and took our time as we didn't want to alert anyone. We got within a few inches and stopped. We would come back that night when the pub was closed. We watched the barman lock up for the night and then made our move.

We got through the wall in minutes, as we had done all the preparation the day before. Once in, we waited and listened for any alarms or cops about. Great! All was good, and then we got to work, first grabbing the cigarettes, cigars, and spirits. Whilst all this stuff was being passed through the hole in the wall by the same crew that had done the soft drinks factory, my brother Thomas is cracking open all the one-arm bandit fruit machines, and James is getting everyone a pint in. Last taken were the beer kegs. We normally would have left them, but we only lived twenty metres from the pub, so two wheel barrows were employed to transport the beer.

We had hides all over the place; the cops had no chance of recovering the goods. Next day we went about the streets and surrounding areas selling all the stuff. We even had a book going to give people time to pay. You must remember that we are only 12 or 14 years old, and the local gang was called the Sally, a bunch of bastards that wouldn't think twice before running a razor down your face. They got wind that we had done the pub, and they tried to get the stuff from us, but we had it hidden all over the place. There was no chance of them bastards getting their hands on it. We made quite a lot of money from that pub.

We are all sitting in the house watching TV and the house below us is being used by the Sally as a drinking den. Most of the houses were empty. My dad had just come in from work, and we could smell smoke. Someone went to the door and opened it, and all this thick, putrid, black, choking smoke poured into our house and filled it in what seemed like seconds.

Thomas ran down the stairs to get help, and in the meantime, my dad got my mother and two sisters out of the house and down the stairs to safety.

This left James and me still in the house. I tried to calm James down and get him out of the house, but he wouldn't leave, so I stayed with him, as there was no way I was leaving him behind. By this time the flames took hold of the landing and were coming up to our house. James tried to jump out the window, and I wrapped my arms round his neck to prevent him from jumping as it was four stories up and it would have been certain death.

We saw all the people in the street, and my mother was screaming at me and James at the window. But there was nothing anyone could do to get to us. The fire brigade were on their way, and I was hoping that they will be here soon. We saw the flames coming up in front of the outside of our window and in the door.

We saw the Sally in the street laughing, as those bastards had deliberately set fire to the house below. I think it was in revenge for not giving them any of the proceeds from the pub job.

We got rescued by the fire brigade, without any injuries.

Again we had to attend another children's panel and were assigned a social worker, a lovely, wee, round woman that cared very much for us. Part of the deal was that we would be given a "dogger's card", which had to be signed by each teacher as we went from each period. We outfoxed them and got Thomas to forge the signatures. This had to be shown to our parents at the end of the day to prove that we had been to school.

Mum and Dad were none the wiser – that is until the authorities caught up with us and sent us back to yet another children's panel, and this time the game was up. I was leaving school officially at age 16, but Thomas and James still had a couple of years to go.

I will never forget that day. It had finally caught up with us, and Thomas and James were taken into care for two years, although they didn't go straight away; they were given a couple of weeks. In the meantime they had to go to a place in the city centre to get kitted out for their new place of residence. Then came the day for them to be taken away. From birth they didn't have a chance; they had spent so long in hospital with illnesses, and now we were being parted again.

The social worker arrived in a large black car with a driver, and she was very gentle with them. Mum was screaming, and I was crying along with my sisters. Thomas and James were quite calm, even though it was one of the worst days of our lives. I watched from the window as they were led into a car, and from that day on, I hated authority. As I write, the tears roll down my face.

Richard Burton

We got to see them most weekends after a couple of months. The two years soon passed, and they were back home again. In June 1976 we moved to Easterhouse in the northwest of Glasgow, where a lot of the people from all over the city were rehoused after the mass demolition and rejuvenation of Glasgow, which was once the second city of the Empire and had built some of the best ships in the world. My dad had been part of that history, having worked on the building of the QE2 at the shipyards. We produced some of the best doctors, scientists, and professors the world had to offer.

How could a city like this be allowed to fall into the abyss? The people started to resent the British establishment, Westminster in particular. During the time I grew up in the 1970s, you were five times more likely to die before the age of 50 in Glasgow than our counterparts in England and Wales.

The narrative in the English press that is always played out is that Scots are drunk and violent, and maybe that much is true, but what is never told is that the reason we are predisposed to violence and drinking has everything to do with poverty and a no-hope society. I have nothing against the English people. I married two Englishwomen, and they gave me three sons. I have two English grandchildren. It's the English system I hate, the arrogance of the Oxbridge, the Etonian snobbery of the stiff collars in an out-of-date institution that still believes it has an empire and hangs on to a belief system of superiority.

As I have said, we moved to Easterhouse in the summer of 1976, and all the windows were smashed in, but it didn't matter as it was recorded as one of the hottest summers in history.

It wasn't long before the news spread that a new family had moved in, and the word about the street was that we were one of the best-looking families. Not for me to say as self-praise is no honour, but everyone wanted to know us. We kept our distance, which added to the intrigue of who we were. We didn't think we were better, but we knew our intellect was higher than the local tribe circling round, waiting for a weakness to appear. As this would be exploited and abused, it was never going to happen. The Burtons were well educated in the law of the jungle.

We eventually got to know the local militia, most of whom were just much the same as us but were going nowhere except prison or the graveyard, because they all belonged to gangs and were out fighting at the weekends and drinking the wine – and I didn't mean the stuff those posh bastards were drinking in the West End, out of a nice glass (we called it electric soup), long before Buckfast Tonic wine. This was your Lanliq or Eldorado, and it got them off their face and into the fighting spirit. It took them away from their existence – until they woke up in a police cell or the hospital.

I only ever wanted to be a soldier. Not only to get away from the rat race of my existence but to be a part of something that was bigger than me. I enlisted into the Territorial army, because at age 16 I tried to join the regular army, but they wouldn't accept me as I was too small and grossly underweight due to years of malnutrition. So I went to the TA Royal Engineers in Coatbridge and enjoyed it very much. But I had to do a selection course, and part of that course was an entrance exam, which I failed as I only had the reading ability of a 10-year-old. I was rejected and told to get further education, so I did.

It started with a couple of nights a week at a local school in Easterhouse. The teacher said to me, "Why don't you apply for full-time education at college?"

I enlisted as a full-time student and got paid the equivalent of dole money plus travelling allowances.

I was at college for about a year and I did very well. In the meantime, I reapplied to join the TA, and this time I went to Maryhill, an infantry regiment of the (RHF) of 1/52 Lowland Volunteers. Some of my best memories were from my time there. In the daytime I attended college, and on nights and weekends I went to the TA.

Soon after, my brother James joined, and we were referred to as the Elvis brothers. During roll call our names weren't mentioned, just the last two of our army numbers, 28 and 56. We had a great time with some brilliant characters, such as old Daniel, the last lamplighter in Glasgow and his pal Sam. The two of them always had a half bottle of whisky in their magazine pouches.

One night after coming home from a disco with a pal, we decided for whatever reason to steal a car. Driving along with no problem, and all of a sudden he lost control of the car. We were only doing about thirty mph, and we hit the pillar of a bridge. All I remember is putting my hands up to my face and that was it. I woke up two days later in hospital, and my dad and a policeman were sitting at my bed.

As soon as I could talk, the policeman said to me, "You are charged with car theft, and a summons will be in the post."

I could tell by the look on Dad's face that I had been quite badly damaged. I had a fractured skull, a broken leg and arm, and fifty-six stitches. I was lucky compared to my pal: he had a broken femur, a punctured valve in his heart, and a collapsed lung, and it was touch-and-go as to whether he would make it. I was 19 and my pal was 17.

We eventually went to court about a year later. I was given a £150 fine and he got a £200 fine, and both of us were banned from driving for two years. The judge told us both that had our injuries not been so bad, we would have been looking at a prison sentence.

I couldn't join the army for at least a year. I continued to attend the TA, and on 20 October 1980, I enlisted into the British army. I passed the entrance exam with flying colours and was told that I scored high enough to join any branch of the army. But all I wanted was the KOSB (King's Own Scottish Borderers), so off I went to Glencorse Barracks in Edinburgh for eighteen weeks of the most intensive training I had seen at that stage in my army career. I passed out of training feeling proud of my achievement. I had finally had my dream come true of something that I had wished for as a very young child.

I joined my battalion on 4 February 1981. We were based in Osnabruck in West Germany, and the battalion was on exercise. It must have been minus ten degrees – very cold winters in Germany – and every day the casualties kept coming into camp with frostbite and trench foot. I know people think it was only World War One where we had trench foot and frostbite, but we had guys go down all the time with the conditions caused by being on long exercises in extreme cold and wet conditions for weeks at a time. I said to myself, "This is the army and not the TA."

MY LIFE IN THE ARMY FROM 1980 TO 1994

As I said previously, I'd always wanted to be a soldier, and now I had made it to my battalion. That was me, one of Britain's finest. The First Battalion King's Own Scottish Borderers was an infantry regiment and part of a large garrison in northwest Germany, namely Osnabruck. If the Russians were ever to attack, our deployment area was a place called Aackma, about three miles from our barracks. We would deploy there as part of a wider NATO force of Britain, France, and of course the United States. This was the spot we would dig in and await the Russian army. We would personally be up against the Third Shock army of a Soviet armoured division of about ten thousand men. We would carry out shoot-and-scoot attacks, paying particular attention to their command and control, taking out commanders and signal vehicles, and basically just trying to disrupt and slow down their advance for long as we could. Our life expectancy was no more than thirty-six hours, giving enough time for re-enforcements to arrive from the United Kingdom. By that time, it was expected that most of us would either be dead or prisoners of war. An unimaginable scenario and one that I am glad was never put into practice.

I loved my time in Germany and long hot summers. I was at the beginning of my service and a very keen and enthusiastic soldier, completing a parachute course, doing six jumps from two thousand feet, and then went onto join the ski team. It was the fittest I have ever been. It set me up for all the other things we had to do all over the world. I spent three years in Germany, and it was there that I practiced my craft of heavy drinking, the ruin of many a good soldier, as the beer was cheap and very strong compared to the British beer of the time.

We left Germany in 1983 to go to Colchester, Essex, where we had quite a reserved reception, as the locals had heard that it was a Scottish regiment that was coming. We were the first Scottish troops in ten years to be posted there, and they hadn't got along with the natives and had beaten a lot of them up and basically trashed the town, so the locals were understandably a bit on edge, especially the publicans. We had heard that we may not be allowed in to some of the bars and that we might get a bit of a frosty reception.

However, we pleasantly surprised the locals, as we weren't quite the savages they thought we were, and soon after we were made most welcome in all the pubs, and the bars were making a fortune out of the jocks. Pretty soon after our arrival the local women started to appear in the pubs, and they were intrigued by our accents, as back then people didn't travel as much as they do today, certainly not within the United Kingdom. We soon had the women eating out of our hands, to the displeasure of the local young bucks, but there wasn't much that they could do about it as there were more of us than them.

I met my first wife down in Colchester, the night I came back from my first tour of Northern Ireland in 1985. It was a bit of a whirlwind romance, married after dating each other for only six months, and she gave birth to my first son on 21 August 1986. We spent four years there, and it was one of the best postings I've ever had. Whilst there I went to Kenya for six weeks. What a magnificent time we had there! It reminded me of the movie *Born Free* starring Virginia McKenna and Bill Travis, a special place that I will always keep in my heart.

We came back from Africa in late November all tanned up and went down the local pubs, and all the women looked at us with white teeth and bronze bodies … oh to be young again! Not long after that we got deployed to a nuclear missile base in Surrey. The Americans had decided to base cruise missiles there at the request of Prime Minister Margaret Thatcher, so all these middle-class housewives with nothing better to do as part of CND descended on the place. We had to patrol the outer fence to stop them from breaking into the compound. We weren't armed, but the Americans on the inner fence were armed to the teeth, and that part of the inner fence was classed as American soil. So if these women got past us and into the American sector, then God only knows what would have happened, as the Americans had orders to open fire, and that was a worry for our head sheds (commanders), and a constant pain in the arse for us.

The last thing we wanted was for one of our own women to be shot by some gung-ho yank.

Early in 1985 we started training for Northern Ireland, my first tour of the province. Over the next two months of intensive training we covered everything that the IRA could possibly throw at us, from sniper attacks to bomb blasts, tripwires, pressure pads, and mortar attacks. Fitness was hammered into our brains, along with patrol skills and lying in OPs (observation posts) for days at a time no matter the weather. We trained until we deployed to South Armagh, one of the deadliest places for a soldier to be during the Troubles. It was a godforsaken place where everyone hated you.

On one of my first patrols I was nearly killed by a thousand pound bomb on the main railway line running from Belfast to Dublin. We were doing a route clearance operation along the track, when all of a sudden we got a reading on our ECM (electronic countermeasure) kit that someone was trying to kill us. Our ECM kept us alive. Bomb disposal arrived and defused it, happy days for now, but there would be many more days like this to come.

Every patrol was fraught with danger that wore on the nerves. It was the never knowing that at any moment it could happen – a sniper's bullet or a bomb. The thing that wore me down the most was parked cars and lampposts. There wasn't a time in my life on the streets of Northern Ireland that preyed on the mind more than the never knowing. The psychology they had over us was unbelievable. We were the hunted and they were the hunters, although if it came to a firefight, we became the dominant force, though those times were few and far between. After a quick burst of automatic gunfire, they would be on their toes over the border into the Irish Republic.

Bear in mind that all my tours were in and around the border areas: South Armagh, East Tyrone, and County Fermanagh, all regarded as "bandit country" and dangerous places. They hated us, and you could taste it. I lost my faith in religion over there, and I was brought up as a devout Catholic. I could see what religion had done to them, so caught up in their own little world of bigotry, so backwards in their approach to the rest of the United Kingdom, of which the Nationalists or Republicans didn't want to be part of.

At the time, as a young soldier, I didn't really understand the politics of it all. I thought I did, but not really. Like most soldiers, we were sent there to do a job, and we did it to the best of our ability. Get the tour over with, and if we didn't lose anyone, then that was the bonus, a tour completed and all back safe.

At the time, the British army was losing quite a lot of men, the average could be as low as five or six or as high as fifteen or twenty, and depending on whether the provost had planned any spectaculars in that year, it could be a large body count. But the general public didn't pay much attention anymore as the Troubles had been with us for so long and was part of our lives.

MY FIRST TOUR OF NORTHERN IRELAND

MARCH TO AUGUST 1985, SOUTH ARMAGH

We arrived at RAF Aldergrove in Belfast from RAF Brize Norton, England. We were taken into a hangar to await helicopters to fly us down to our respective locations. Inside the hangar, this old lady who worked as a volunteer for the WRVS (women's royal voluntary service), who must have been in her late 70s, handed out little cards with prayers on them to help keep us safe for the duration of our tour. I found this very humbling, as she kept saying, "God bless you all." She had been doing this for every regiment since the Troubles started in 1969 and had been threatened by the IRA on numerous occasions. She died about twenty years ago and was given an MBE for her services.

I was part of the Mortar Platoon, Support Company, One KOSB. About thirty-six strong, we deployed to Forkhill, about two hundred metres from the border with the republic, so a very dangerous place. We took over from Second Battalion, the Parachute Regiment. We flew down in waves of three and a couple of Lynx helicopters doing top cover to protect us from ground attack, as the IRA was capable of bringing down a chopper.

On arrival, as we disembarked from the helicopters, the PARAS were straight on them, handover complete. Speed is of the essence as the longer the chopper is on the helipad, the greater the chance of being mortared. As soon as the whole platoon was in location, it was a case of grab a quick mug of tea and an egg sandwich, then straight to the briefing room for an intelligence briefing, a job that many more years later I would go on to do. A quick brief on the threat and past incidents and then tasked with what your multiple is assigned to do. (A multiple is three teams of four men, a total of twelve, each patrolling and supporting one another on the ground. No patrol goes out on the ground with fewer than twelve men.) Our multiple was tasked with sanger duty. A sanger is the watchtower of the base, so it was a nice, easy job to start with, to ease us in to being over there, as we were shitting ourselves and didn't really know what to expect.

The tour started off quietly with nothing happening. This day we got intelligence that the base was going to be attacked by the IRA, so we got deployed to the surrounding area in a covert role and lay in wait for them to attack. Then we would hit them. I was in this barn with the rest of my team. We had been there two days, and we had to shit in cling film and piss in milk containers. No smoking and no hot food – it's called hard routine.

I was sitting on my bergan (rucksack) with my rifle across my knees and looking through the crack on the stable door, listening to the crackle of the radio in my earpiece. The other three guys are asleep. All of a sudden the farmer turns up and comes straight up to the door. I'm sitting there on the other side of it, with my rifle pointing straight at his chest, not making a sound and just staring at him, not even blinking, that's how close I was to this old bastard. He fucked off and I immediately woke up my team commander, a veteran of previous tours, and told him that I thought we might have been compromised. We got the other two up. We sorted out our kits and got ready to bug out. The IRA can mount an attack in fifteen minutes.

We heard this almighty explosion, and then the shockwaves hit us. We looked at each other and said, "Fuck, the base has been hit!" which was only about two hundred metres from us. The radios blasted out all sorts of shite, and all this radio traffic was coming over the net. We were told to get to the next field and that a chopper was inbound to pick us up. Still unsure what happened yet, my team commander was trying to get details from the OPs room (operations room). He told us a bomb had been detonated on the main Belfast to Dublin Road, against an RUC (police) mobile patrol.

This was my first incident, and what a fucking mess! As I approached the area, all I could see from the helicopter was a massive crater and the mangled wreckage of what was once a car and a hay truck. We landed and immediately got a cordon around the bomb site. Bits of broken bodies were scattered all over the place: legs, arms, and torsos. All the SOCO (scenes of crime officers) teams arrived and did their forensic search and evidence

It Cuts Me Deeply

gathering, and then the recovery of the body parts began. We didn't do that, the police did. They just put them into clear plastic bags and took them away.

Four police officers had been killed in the explosion, one being a woman. The problem was that they couldn't find her head, so we got tasked to search for it, but we never did find it. It either evaporated in the explosion or some wildlife ran away with it. Just three months before this incident, nine police officers were killed when the IRA mortared the Newry police station whilst they were having breakfast. I saw a photo of the policewoman who was killed. She was 23 years old, and it was gut-wrenching to see how young and pretty she was.

Not long after, we got mortared at a lookout post overlooking Newry called "Super Bowl." Two days before, a well-known IRA man was seen pacing out the field below. This was the brigade commander for the Sough Armagh PIRA (provisional Irish Republican army), and it was his land. You must remember all these IRA men had plenty of money in South Armagh. They are mainly farmers and owned all the land, so if they happened to be out and about on that land, no one could question them as to why they were there. It happened at four o'clock. Six mortar rounds came thumping into the position. There were pre-dug trenches that had a lid on them and they looked like coffins. Each man had to get inside these things when mortared. Fuck that! That was too much. We preferred to get behind a sandbag wall. Two of the rounds overshot and two dropped short and two landed right in the middle of the position. Not much damage and no one hurt.

A couple of weeks later same location and A Company are up on the Super Bowl doing a routine base plate patrol, meaning doing perimeter patrol. They came down the mountain and patrolled the road. There was a hay truck at the side of the road, so they decided to give it a wide berth and go round the outside of it. It is a good job that they did as just as they drew level, it exploded. If they had come up the other side, they would all have been killed. There were minor injuries, and one guy lost an eye.

Then the base at Crossmaglen got mortared as the chopper was coming in to lift out members of B Company. As the chopper landed, two rounds were fired into the base, and the CSM (company sergeant major) got shrapnel wounds to his back while trying to save one of the jocks who was

Richard Burton

about to get on the chopper. We never lost anyone on that tour, but it was my first tour of Northern Ireland, and from that day on I hated the Irish. There would be many more times that I would have to face these people.

We came back from Northern Ireland in August 1985, and I felt proud. I was now a veteran and one of the boys. Sitting in the pub with the guys, I and my team commander and my pal Ian were having a party at his girlfriend Shirley's house. We were contemplating whether to go to this party, as we are going on leave the next day. We decided to go, and when we arrived, all the jocks were there. This girl was talking to one of the MOW (Men of War).

As soon as I walked in, Shirley pulled her away from the guy and said, "Sarah, this is Richard, the guy I've been telling you about."

We got talking and ended up together most of the night. We chatted and kissed. She was going on holiday the next day, and I was going on leave, so we ended it that night.

My pal stayed down in Colchester for a couple of weeks and then came up to Glasgow. We went out for a drink, and he said to me, "I have that girl's phone number. You have to call her. I think she likes you."

So when I got back to Colchester, I gave her a call at her mum and dad's, and we arranged to meet up and start dating. It was a messy beginning, as she had been dating Shirley's brother, Sam. The first inkling I had of this was when we were driving through Colchester and she panicked, as he was in a car behind us.

I said, "Who is this guy?" and she said, "It's Shirley's brother, and he's a nasty piece of work."

Unaware that she had been seeing him at the same time she had been seeing me, it sorted itself out when she told him she wanted nothing more to do with him. Sam wasn't too happy about this and always resented me, as I had taken another lady away from him a year before that (back then I was quite a catch). It all came to a head at Shirley's 21st birthday party and all the jocks were there, mainly the mortar platoon and the anti-tank platoon.

I was arguing with Sarah out in the corridor of the venue and Sam got involved. I told him to piss off before he got hurt – I was fitter than any one of these mugs. I hooked him and down he went. Before you knew it the

It Cuts Me Deeply

place erupted, and it was a full-scale battle, the jocks against the English, and what a battle it was.

Sam had all the would-be hard men of Essex's gangsters there, but they just hadn't come up against the jocks before, and every one of them got a hiding of their lives. Even the police congratulated us for sorting them out, as all these arseholes were well known to them.

As I said, I and Sarah had a whirlwind romance and married on 21 December 1985. I was due to get married and going on Christmas leave when word came down from Battalion HQ that the battalion was to form outside on the parade square. We were then told by the commanding officer that we had been put on twenty-four-hour notice to deploy to Northern Ireland, as it had kicked off over there. We and the Royal Anglian Regiment, whom we shared a camp with, would be deploying over there within the next twenty-four hours, so leave was put on hold. I had to get permission to leave camp to get married at Colchester register office. Permission was granted, and the wedding went ahead, and we ended up not deploying to Northern Ireland until January 1986 for a two-month emergency tour. The KOSB went to Omagh, and the Royal Anglian Regiment went to Londonderry. My Company went to the Maze Prison and used it as a patrol base. We had been sent to Northern Ireland to protect the prison officers, as quite a few had been killed by the IRA.

We then deployed to St Lucia barracks in Omagh along with B Company and started to do patrols in and around that TAOR (tactical area of responsibility). This night, a guy in his 50s came into our camp and went straight into the office of his company commander of the UDR (Ulster defence regiment). He was told that the IRA was going to assassinate him and that he should be very careful whilst at his workplace. He worked for the council cleaning out the drains.

Our multiple was to shadow him as he went about his job of cleaning the drains. He was a part-time member of the UDR and had just pulled into a sewage depot and was cleaning out the tanks. We patrolled past him and gave him a nod to let him know we were there. We crossed the road and up onto the high ground to do an overwatch. Just as we got to the top of the hill I heard automatic gunfire. As I turned round to look I saw two IRA men firing a burst into his face. He immediately fell back, and we couldn't return fire as we were too far away and it would have meant firing across a busy duel carriageway. We ran as fast as we could to close with the enemy, but they were off in seconds in a car.

As I approached him, he was lying on his back, and the whole left side of his face was missing. He lay there in a massive pool of blood and was clearly dead. I will never forget or stop blaming myself for the fact that just maybe if we had been that little bit closer or even if we had returned fire, it might have caused the IRA execution squad to panic long enough for us to save this man's life. I will never forget him, even though I didn't know him personally. All agencies were tasked and a major search operation went into action, but the assassins were never found.

We came back from Northern Ireland, and I carried on with a happy marriage. My first son was born 21 August 1986.

In 1989, my third tour of Northern Ireland, I was working with the battalion intelligence section. It was my job to collate intelligence and brief patrols before they went out on the ground. It was a hard tour –cold, wet, and snowing. During Christmas and the new year, we deployed on September 1989 until March 1990.

On 13 December 1989, intelligence came through that one of the checkpoints along the border was going to be attacked. The only problem was, we didn't know which one. So a quick appreciation was studied by the boffins, and they said it was Derryard, as it was closest to the Monaghan border and the least defended.

On the morning of 13 December, it was decided to send down another multiple from support company to beef up and strengthen the checkpoint. I briefed them at ten that morning, and off they went to Derryard. One of the soldiers I'd briefed was killed. He had just come back from R and R the day before it.

At approximately 4.20, I was sitting in the int cell when all of a sudden the radio came alive with a contact report, and in between message I heard a lot of automatic gunfire in the background. We didn't know the extent of the attack or if we had any casualties at this stage, I heard clearly my pal speaking on the radio to the battalion OPS officer. We then heard that we had one casualty. At this point the quick reaction force was in the sky in a chopper and on its way to the checkpoint. The IRA had attacked using a cement truck and their numbers were eighteen. They drove up to the checkpoint, and as the soldier approached the truck, the driver sounded his

It Cuts Me Deeply

horn. That was the signal for a gunman in the back of the truck to shoot him once in the head and twice in the chest. He died immediately. At the same time, another IRA man fired an RPG (rocket-propelled grenade) at the sanger. It collapsed, and another soldier on the ground was injured. They then reversed the truck through the gates of the checkpoint and disembarked, firing a flamethrower through the command sanger where Bobby was. They threw a grenade at the injured soldier and he managed to kick it away, causing shrapnel wounds to his back and legs.

Another soldier, who was on rest at the time, thought the checkpoint was being mortared. He ordered his guys to get their body armour and helmets on and to get under their beds, as was the drill for a mortar attack. He went outside to see what was happening, and he ran straight into a hail of automatic gunfire. It hit him on the side of the head, killing him instantly.

The IRA continued to clear all the buildings with grenades and gunfire. Another soldier was trapped in the canteen. He'd been making a brew for the guys when the attack happened. He didn't have his rifle with him. The IRA were spraying the whole compound with automatic gunfire and throwing grenades. They threw a grenade inside the canteen, and he hid between the cooker and the fridge. The grenade landed between his legs but failed to explode. He was never the same and left the army shortly after.

By this time the team commander, my brother-in-law of the time, and his patrol were out on an external patrol and heard the gunfire. They rushed down from the high ground and onto the road and straight into a hail of gunfire from the IRA men on the back of the truck. A firefight ensued and the terrorist started to withdraw, but before doing so, they drove a red van onto the base. It had a five hundred-pound bomb on board, and in their haste to prime the bomb whilst under fire, they only had time to prime the booster charge, so thankfully the bomb didn't explode or we would have lost everyone that day.

It was the largest single attack that the IRA had ever mounted against a British army checkpoint in Northern Ireland. We had two dead and one wounded, and for their actions on that day, both commanders were awarded the DCM (distinguished conduct medal) from the queen at Buckingham Palace. Another soldier was awarded a posthumous mention in despatches. Personally, I think all of them should have been recognised for their bravery that day.

At the end of the tour, Three PARA (Third Battalion, Parachute Regiment) were taking over from us. I had to take their team commanders and company commanders out on a familiarisation patrol of the area.

I said, "Let's go to this house, and I'll introduce to one of the bastards that was part of the IRA active service unit at Derryard."

He opened the door – a short, stocky, blond-haired guy that was one bad bastard.

My next tour of the province was 1992–94, and back to our old stomping ground of South Armagh, this time Crossmaglen, the most dangerous place in the whole of Northern Ireland. You really had to be on your toes in that place – take your eye off the ball for a second and you were a dead man. I hated that place.

I was on a patrol in and around the town, and our patrol turned down an alley. We got a reading on our ECM kit (nicknamed the Violet Joker), and it started to sound off attack. I was twenty metres away from the car bomb. Another piece of our ECM kit called the Antler was stopping the bomb from detonating.

The IRA was lying in wait on top of the hill in the graveyard, trying to detonate the bomb. It was a terrible tour, and it was the very last tour I would ever do of Northern Ireland, as I left the army later that year. To think I could have been killed. Many years later, that car and that day would feature in my nightmares.

Two days after that incident, one of our checkpoints was mortared, and my best friend was injured. Another guy was badly injured. I stood in a shop doorway and watched the choppers going into the checkpoint to lift out the casualties.

Three little boys about 10 years old came up to me and said, "You'll be needing plenty of condolence cards tonight, jock."

What could I do? They were only kids. I turned towards the doorway and the tears ran down my face. That place haunts me to this day.

I have often thought of going back to Northern Ireland as a civilian and walking round some of the places I patrolled as a soldier, to try and put some ghosts to rest, but I really don't know if I could cope with it.

As soon as I hear an Irish brogue, it makes the hairs on my neck stand up. Today is the fiftieth anniversary of British troops being deployed to Northern Ireland as part of Operation Banner, the longest single deployment ever in thirty-eight years. More than 1,441 soldiers were killed and more than six thousand were wounded. Countless others were psychologically damaged (PTSD, among other illnesses), myself included.

We got some things wrong over there, but we got more things right. We are one of the most professional and most disciplined armies in the world, and us being there saved thousands of lives of what would have been a full-scale civil war. Was it worth it? Yes, I think so. Many people are walking about alive today because of what we did.

Will there be lasting peace over there? I'm not so sure. With all this Brexit and the Irish backstop, they don't need many excuses to kick things off again, it's too ingrained in their DNA. All I know for sure is that I won't be any part of it.

In between tours of Northern Ireland, Saddam Hussain decided to invade Kuwait in August 1990, so a rapid response was required from the West and in particular the United States and its little dog, Britain. All the armoured divisions from Germany went first. We were still going about our normal duties in Edinburgh. In fact, I spent six weeks in the United States and six weeks in Jamaica. I came back, went on Christmas leave, picked up my son, and spent my leave at my mum and dad's over the New Year's period. All was going great and had a great time with my son and a good new year with the family.

On New Year's Day, the police came to the door and asked my dad if I was there. I went to the door and was told I had to report to barracks as my regiment had been recalled and that I had to report back immediately. Jesus, it was 1 January, and I had no way of getting my son back until 3 January, as there would be no trains going to London until then. I called the sergeant major and explained, and he was fine with it as long as I kept him updated.

I got my son back on 3 January 1991 and then made my way to Redford barracks in Edinburgh. The snow was about eighteen inches deep and it was freezing. I got to the camp, and all the vehicles are on the parade square, painted in desert colours, just sitting there waiting to be transported to South Hampton for the four-week journey to the Middle East. I got into the lines (living accommodations), and the place was abuzz with a hive of activity – guys getting issued desert kits and all sorts of things going on.

I was told I was going to Charlie Company as I had just been busted to private again. OK, we are off to war and all hands are needed and that old jazz. I reported to the company and was part of Seven Platoon. I was given the task as platoon signaller, as I was the most experienced with the radio. I got myself a bunk and sorted out my kit, bergan, and my webbing (fighting order).

We then started off with ten days of preparing for war: that is, fitness at 05.30 in the morning in the snow, then breakfast, after that lectures on NBC (nuclear, biological, and chemical warfare), first aid, handling of POWs, and a briefing on the Geneva Conventions. We all had to report to the medical centre to get our jabs, which consisted of anthrax, bubonic plague, typhoid, and a number of other shite of which we had no idea of what it was. And today, many guys have died and are still dying as a result of the stuff they gave us. It's called Gulf War syndrome. We deployed to the Gulf on 16 January 1991 in the early hours of the morning, and all the media were there, including Scottish television and the BBC.

The camp was white with snow, and as we drove out, I looked back at Redford barracks and said to myself, "I might never see this place again," and thought of how many of us might not return.

We arrived at RAF Brize Norton to catch our flights to Saudi Arabia. We were there for about ten hours before our flights were due to leave, so all the card games started to appear. One of the guys gave everyone a haircut, number ones all over, at the cost of £1 per skull. He must have made a fortune, although the money was to go to company funds. Aye right, knowing him, maybe a third of that made it to the company funds – no offence, pal.

On arrival at Saudi, the door of the aircraft opened and the heat was intense and unbearable. As we left the aircraft, each man was given a bottle of water. As we headed towards the hangars for final processing, I looked along the airport, and as far as the eye could see, the amount of fighter jets and apache gunships seemed to go on for miles. I had never seen so much firepower in all my time in the army.

No sooner did I digest all of this than a loud wailing noise of the sirens alerted us that a Scud missile was coming towards us. We actually saw it go right over head towards Israel. Welcome to Saudi!

We continued with our training and a period of acclimatising, so each night we had Scud alerts and watched them as they headed for Israel. The American Patriot missiles would intercept them, although some did get through and hit Israel. The world held its breath as Saddam Hussain tried to draw Israel into the war. If he succeeded, the coalition would crumble, as no Arab nation would be on the side of Israel. Therefore, Saudi Arabia would back down and we would have no ground base in the Middle East in which to launch an attack to liberate Kuwait. This would be a disaster and a possible annexation of Kuwait by Saddam Husain, a foothold on the world's oil supply and an end to the markets of the United States on its control of the Middle East and the collapse of the global economy. There was a possibility of it becoming a global conflict in the region and a world war. Against the whole Arab nation, without oil, the West would be crippled and the war machine of the American military industrial complex was having to rely on its own oil reserves to fight a war thousands of miles away. Israel could not come into this war, so cue the British SAS. They were our only hope to save this war from becoming a catastrophe.

General Norman Schwarzkopf wasn't keen on special forces as he'd had bad experiences with them in Vietnam, until Peter de la Billière, commander of UK forces in the Gulf, told him that it was British special forces and the SAS. Schwarzkopf remembered how well they had done in the desert in 1944 under David Stirling and Blair "Paddy" Maine, and he eventually agreed to hand control of knocking out the Scuds to the SAS.

Whilst all this is going on without our knowledge, we were training in a place called Devil Dog Dragoon Ranges in the middle of the desert in extreme heat, carrying out section and platoon attacks, using live ammunition and no safety pamphlet (which governs safety during peacetime on the range). This doesn't apply during wartime training, so if guys are killed, that is classed as an acceptable loss.

We had rounds flying over our heads and guys throwing grenades and bayonets fixed; the adrenaline rush was at its highest as we really got psyched up to killing the enemy. It was a state of euphoria I have never experienced since.

When the training finished, it was time to get prepared for battle. The

SAS had done their job, and now it was down to us to get into Iraq and puncture the Republican Guard and push like hell towards Kuwait. The order came on 24 February 1991, just after midnight, and I was thinking of my son and then of my mother and father and the rest of the family. Would I ever see them again? It's what I had trained for all my life, and now I was getting tested. Did I have the guts, or was I a bottle merchant? In my mind I would never let my family down, especially my great-uncle, who had been killed in World War 1, and my grandfather, who had been badly wounded in the same battle of Nueve Chapel in 1915.

We drove 140 miles west and then north towards the Iraqi border. It's the breach (us breaking through the Iraqi front lines). This was it, and the gunfire got louder, and the aircraft bombardment was so loud it was hard to hear anything else. The sky was ablaze, and I couldn't believe it had started to snow, more like sleet, and the temperature has dropped. We were lucky to have our warm kit with us, unlike the SAS (two had frozen to death). The bombardment was heavier than the bombing of Dresden in the Second World War.

We crossed the border and started to see the dead. The very first guy I saw was hanging out of a trench, and he didn't exist from his waist down. As I went deeper into Iraq, the body count became greater and my brain was trying to process it all. I never really spoke about the impact that the war had on me, or what I later became and the diabolical situation I ended up in caused by a war that none of us really wanted to be part of.

When I reached the Basra Road, also known as the Highway of Death, I had never seen so much devastation in all my life. I couldn't comprehend it. The place was mangled with dead bodies that were now decomposing. It is estimated that about ten thousand had perished. It was an unprecedented number, and the sad fact was that I was becoming immune to it. There I was walking amongst the dead as if they didn't matter. What was I becoming? I was part of the machine that had destroyed them. I was so removed from the reality that had created this carnage and horror on the human race.

Unfortunately, I had become conditioned to the horrors of war, as so many of our predecessors had in wars past. It's the human brain's coping mechanism for dealing with things that we should never see or be exposed to. I was a little more equipped to deal with violent sights than other members of the battalion, as I grew up seeing stabbings and guys get chopped to pieces in the gang fights of Glasgow.

We started to take prisoners of war very quickly; so many of them just came out of their trenches waving white flags, shaking and crying and hoping we wouldn't shoot them. We had bayonets fixed and pointing at them to get on the ground, as we had to take control and keep them in the shock of capture. You must remember that they were still the enemy and could attack and kill us at any time.

We searched them and passed them along to an area in the desert, with white mine tape as a pen for them to sit in. It was still snowing, more like sleet than snow, and some of these guys were wounded, and many of them had no boots or socks on and had been getting bombed day and night constantly for six weeks. They were a terrible mess. The Red Cross turned up with doctors and proper medical equipment, and we gave the prisoners tarpaulin to cover themselves to keep the snow and wind off. Medics past round a tube of grip bandages for their feet, and hot tea was given to them.

We dug pits at the corner of the pens for them to do the toilet and the prisoners screamed and grabbed our hands and kissed our feet. We quickly realised they thought we were digging their graves, so we had to get an Iraqi that could speak English to translate what the pit was for. Eventually everyone calmed down.

I was told to take this one Iraqi over to the field doctor for treatment, as he had a bad injury to his head and needed it looked at. I pointed my rifle at him, with bayonet fixed and gestured for him to stand up. He got up very frightened as he didn't know if he was to be shot. Their dictators had told them that if the British or Americans captured them, they would all be killed. I got him to the doctor, and the guy was so scared he wouldn't let the doctor examine him. He was given a carton of apple juice, and I gave him a bar of chocolate, and this seemed to calm him down. He needed a lot of stitches to the head wound, and when the doctor removed the guy's trousers, he and I couldn't believe the amount of lice that were crawling all over him. His legs had become ulcerated and riddled with scabies, and the doctor told me to tell my men that when handling these prisoners to make sure we all wore gloves.

We held on to them, about five hundred in total, until first light, which was about 4.30, until the Chinook helicopters came in to take them to a

Saudi POW camp called Maryhill Camp, as it had been built and set up by the RHF (Royal Highland Fusiliers). The RHF and KOSB had initially been tasked as POW guard forces, but when we arrived, the battle order had changed. So the pipe band of both regiments were to do prison camp guard force.

After the prisoners got lifted out, we got back on the vehicles and continued with our next task. We heard that the Republican Guard Tank Division was heading towards us and the company commander said, "I hope that our tanks get to them before they get to us or we will be wiped out as a battalion."

We were an infantry regiment and didn't have the equipment to fight tanks, we fought ground troops. We went firm and dug in and prepared for the worst and waited. In the far distance we could hear that a major tank battle was taking place, and thankfully our tanks had engaged the Republican Guard Tanks and got to them before they got to us. The battle raged on for about five or six hours, and we just sat there watching and listening in between guys trying to get some sleep. You must rest in war whenever possible, as you don't know when your next chance to sleep will come.

We eventually got the order to move to where the tank battle had taken place, and we were told to engage any enemy that was still there and still willing to fight. By the time we got there, it was a scene of complete and utter devastation. It was like hell, just a battlefield littered with burnt-out tanks and the charred remains of what was once some mother's son or someone's father. It was an eye opener, and this was before I had even reached the Basra Road.

We dug in right in front of the tank graveyard and got a brew on and had something to eat. People back home would find this hard to believe or think we were just animals, but such is war. The guys were quiet and withdrawn, as each of us knew that if our tanks hadn't engaged with them, it would be our charred remains.

The ground offensive only lasted one hundred hours, but the devastation I had seen in four days would be imprinted on my mind forever. I will never forget the sights that I witnessed, but the smell also stays with me, so much so that I couldn't eat bacon or any kind of pork for about ten years, as the smell reminded me of burning flesh.

It Cuts Me Deeply

We came back from the Gulf War in June 1991 to Edinburgh Airport and to a large crowd all cheering and waving flags. As we walked down the steps of the aircraft, it was everyone's wives, children, and girlfriends, and it was emotional.

Ian, one of my best pals at the time, said to me, "Richard, that's not for me or you; there won't be anybody out there for us, pal."

As I walked through the gates of Edinburgh Airport and all the guys are hugging their wives and children and the single guys are hugging their girlfriends, Ian and I just walked straight past them and jumped on our bus (separate buses for the single soldiers and another bus for the married men and their partners).

We arrived at Redford barracks and a drink had been laid on courtesy of a local brewery. I was walking towards the cookhouse, and my sister Annette was there. She had been at the airport but I missed her. She was there with her in-laws and would have been there to see her husband coming back.

I ended up at Annette's that night, getting drunk as you do, but I wanted to go back to barracks, so the next day I went back and it was empty, as everyone was on leave. I went to my room after getting my kit out of the stores, as all my civilian clothes were in a box. I got into my room and heard this groaning in the corner.

I looked round the locker, and Ian was lying in bed in the room we shared. He said, "How did it go at Annette's last night?"

I said, "It was good," but my mind was still on the Basra Road and the tank graveyard, and it was hard to get my head away from it, and it was best that I was back in camp.

So I got my suit out of the box, took off my desert kit, had a shower, and headed into Edinburgh with my pal. We went into this pub, quite a posh bar, and we stood at the bar. This woman was talking to her partner about curtains and carpets or something of that description and we just stood there listening to this. We both felt like grabbing them and throwing them out the window, but you couldn't do that.

They had no idea of what we had just been through. We had changed, and I knew that the minute I walked through the gates at Edinburgh Airport. It would never be the same again, even though we didn't kill a single Iraqi, and I am so glad of that as I have enough demons going on in my head. But we had been traumatised by the very nature of our experiences.

We continued with our leave, going on the drink for about a week or so, and then I went down to London to pick up my son who was about 5 at the time. Not knowing at the time, fifteen years later he would go on to fight in Iraq and Afghanistan and see much more than I ever did. So proud of him.

We left Edinburgh that year and were posted to Weeton barracks, Lancashire, just outside Blackpool and were told that it would be a staging post for deployment to Northern Ireland and that it would be for two years, with two companies in and two companies out at a time and would rotate every six weeks.

Back into our old stomping ground of South Armagh, East Tyrone, and County Fermanagh. As I've said before, all very dangerous places and a high casualty rate for British soldiers. We would face the Barrett Sniper, who had killed nine soldiers in about a year and there was no way of stopping this bastard. The SAS had been deployed to catch him, but the guy was killing from about one kilometre away and firing from the back of a car. It was always close to the border with the Irish Republic. British soldiers were dropping like flies, and it was beginning to wear us down.

The last soldier he killed was at a checkpoint in Bessbrook, South Armagh, before his capture by the SAS in 1997. He was also responsible for the Canary Wharf bombing of the financial district of London. And got sentenced to ninety-nine years in prison and laughed at the judge as he was taken down. He served eighteen months and was released as part of the Good Friday agreement but died two years later of cancer, so we got some justice.

We continued to patrol Northern Ireland for the next two years, and I saw the change in the battalion. The drinking was getting worse, and the violence and domestic problems amongst the married soldiers got worse, including my sister with her husband.

I broke into the cookhouse on Christmas Eve. I had just come back from Northern Ireland that night and had gone into Blackpool for a drink. Even though we were confined to camp, by then I knew something was seriously wrong with me. It wasn't just Northern Ireland or the Gulf War, it was a culmination of my whole life that was beginning to catch up with me and I knew it. But you couldn't say that your mind was affected by your service or it would be career over and you would be out the door. That's just the way it was then.

I didn't only steal meat, I wrecked the cookhouse and smashed all the plates and anything that I could get my hands on, and then I went about the camp leaving meat parcels all over the place and filled my room with chickens, bacon, and sausages. he guys still talk about it and laugh to this day. But the reason I did it was a throwback to my childhood of hunger; I was drunk and was hungry and wanted food and the cookhouse was there.

I was discovered in my room the next morning lying in my bed cuddling a very large chicken and one sitting on top of my TV. I was locked up in the guard room and held for seven days and went up in front of the commanding officer and was reduced in the ranks again.

I was posted back to a rifle company, now 34 years of age. I said to myself, "It's time to go," so I handed in my notice. It normally was a year's notice, but a trial period of a six months' notice was being tested, so I jumped on that right away. I was due to leave the army in August, but I was hit by a car and broke my leg, so I had to remain in the army until I was fit enough to pass my medical.

At this time I took my first overdose and was taken to hospital and kept overnight. They wanted me to see the psychiatrist, but the army was having none of it and sent the MO (medical officer) to the hospital and told them the army would take care of any mental-health problems I had, so I was immediately released back into the army's care.

I was taken straight back to camp and put in front of the RSM (regimental sergeant major). I hated this guy, and he didn't like me either. I stood there with my leg in plaster, and he told me to get a grip and man up. I lost it and offered him a square go, so I was locked up for three days. That's how the army treated someone who just tried to take his own life. Led by idiots, they were no better at soldering than I was, but they never went against the system and climbed the ranks.

I sat in my room on this Sunday evening and I had just had my plaster off on the Friday.

One of my mates said, "Do want to go into Blackpool for a drink?"

I said, "Why not?" By this time I didn't have to attend any muster parades, as all my kit had been handed in.

We went into a pub that was out of bounds to soldiers, as apparently drugs were being dealt there. I had to laugh at these idiots – tell me a pub in Blackpool that wasn't dealing drugs. This was where I met Barbara, who I would go on to marry.

If I hadn't broken my leg, I would have been out of the army six weeks earlier, and we never would have met, and my sons would not have been born.

We had a great time and met up the next night, and I told her that I was leaving the army in about two weeks and that I would be returning to Glasgow and that a relationship was out of the question. But we continued to see each other for the next two weeks.

I returned to Glasgow and then had to get a house. I had been on the council waiting list for years and got a great house, a four in a block with great neighbours, but I got a message from my sister Annette that I had to call Barbara straight away.

So I called her and she told me that she was pregnant, and she asked me what I intended to do. Although it was a shock and wasn't what we had both planned, I said that I would do the right thing by her. So I went down to Blackpool and spent the weekend and discussed it. She was living at her friend's house, and it was never going to be a permanent situation.

I said, "I've just been given a two-bedroom house, and it's a permanent address." I suggested she come up with me and see it and have a look around Glasgow too, as I knew the English got all the bad press about being the knife capital of Europe. She did and was very pleased to come up.

I arranged a van and went down and picked up her belongings. My mother was dying of cancer at the time, so I left Barbara's mum's phone number with my brother James. I had no sooner got into Barbara's mum's and the phone rang and it was my brother James telling me our mother had passed away about half an hour earlier. There was nothing I could do. It was the same when my dad had died and I was in Northern Ireland. It's just the way life is, and I had to suck it up.

We got back to Glasgow the next day and unloaded the van and then headed to my brother James's house to make the arrangements. My other brother Thomas had already taken care of everything.

I didn't cry when I looked at my mother in her coffin, and I didn't realise why for many years after. The reason why goes all the way back to me visiting her in hospital and missing her and having to visit my brothers and sister. She had been through so much pain in her life, with illness, poverty, and alcoholism, and this was the end of the road and the end of the pain and suffering. This good-looking woman had endured so much in her short 63 years on this earth. In spite of the poverty we suffered and the abuse of drink-fuelled violence, we knew this was all a mirror of pain and that pain was projected onto us. We felt the consequences of that pain and hunger and awful living conditions and Thomas and James being taken away. But I will always love my mother, and through all her faults, she was a good woman with a beautiful heart that belonged to a generation of women that didn't give in no matter what. We would always be together as a family. Her fight with alcohol got harder as time went on, and we were beginning to grow up and leave the nest. She was no longer the matriarch of the family, so at the end she was left with nothing. My dad had already passed away three years earlier, and all she had left was memories. At the end she didn't even have them left, and as the cancer took hold, she stopped smoking and drinking. I remember looking at her, and it was the healthiest she had looked in such a long time, but she was dying.

"Man's search for meaning to live is to suffer, to survive is to find meaning in the suffering."

Viktor Frankl, Concentration Camp Survivor

Yet we continue with life, and the pain of my personal journey never ends. I moved to Lancashire in 2000 and bought a house and settled in. I had a job at British Aerospace doing security of the site, where Euro fighters were being built and the repairs of the Harrier and Tornado fighter jets were being made. I actually sat inside these aircraft and many other things that I have done in my life that most people wouldn't believe, but it doesn't matter as I know them to be true. I have guarded Rudolph Hess, Adolph Hitler's right-hand man and deputy Führer whilst he was held at Spandau Prison in Berlin. I have met the queen and once served her dinner at the Berlin Allied Forces Day parade. I did protection for the judges and barristers at Craigavon Court in Northern Ireland, and it wasn't until my trial at Court that the prosecution barrister mentioned it to the Judge that he remembered that the KOSB were protecting the court whilst IRA Terrorists stood trial. He said he found it uncomfortable to be prosecuting a man that had once protected him, so that the due process of law could take place.

My mental state was beginning to diminish soon after arriving in Poulton, and I also felt that Barbara was beginning to distance herself from me, as I was becoming an embarrassment in drink and talking rubbish and making up all sorts of stories about myself. When I look back with embarrassment and wonder why, the answer came to me when I was in the psychiatric hospital. It was based on low self-esteem, not climbing the ranks in the army, and a degenerative childhood of never feeling good enough. And trauma transcends generations – that was how Mother's trauma had transferred itself on to us. Brain trauma starts in the womb, and that reflects how we become as adults, and that continues throughout generations of good people who end up screwed up through no fault of their own. If you're not strong enough to get through life, it will destroy you and turn you into either a drunk or violent, abusive partner, and that is why I must take absolute responsibility for the wrongs that I have done in my life. No one is to blame for my actions except me. I'm glad both my wives got rid of me, as at least my sons had a chance of a good upbringing without a violent drunk like me.

I have said that I'm a good person, but I'm a very damaged person who could never be a good parent with good guidance, and that's what both these women saw in me, and I had to be gone. As Ian once said to me, "Why have all the women that you have ever been in a relationship with walked out on you?" He was right. They can't all be wrong, so who is the common denominator? Me. Why am I putting myself down? Because I am speaking the truth. I would love to be the person that people see on the surface, but it's not who I am. I'm bad tempered, moody, jealous, insecure, and a controlling partner. And that's why I choose to be alone and why no woman deserves to be with me. I will probably die alone. I wish things could have been different, I really do, but it wasn't to be. I don't have many more years left now and thank God, because this life has been a hard struggle of pretence and agony, and it has taken all the struggles of this life to come to terms with what is in front of me. Unlike my mother, who didn't ever speak about how she truly felt, I have been and am sorry for the pain I have caused others. I can't change it and can't undo the damage I've done. All I can say to those I have hurt is sorry.

FROM PSYCHIATRIC HOSPITAL TO COMPLETE RECLUSE AND ISOLATION

Condemnation without investigation is the height of ignorance.
Albert Einstein

My mental state was continuing to deteriorate, and I wasn't receiving any help, although I had been diagnosed with PTSD eight years previously in 1996 and was in receipt of a war pension for that diagnosis. I was drinking heavier but was still working and holding it together and trying so hard to be a husband and father, but the fight was unbearable, the nightmares were getting worse, and now I was having flashbacks of Northern Ireland and the Gulf War. None of them made any sense; they seemed to be mushed together, and some of the things that didn't happen were in there too.

It was driving me crazy and I couldn't cope. Every time there was a sudden bang or a helicopter in the sky I was immediately back on the streets of Northern Ireland. I went to my GP and was given the obligatory antidepressants to calm me down and help with my sleep. The doctor wrote to a well-known military charity, and I was invited for two weeks for an inpatient assessment. And at the end of the assessment I was further diagnosed with PTSD at the severe level of the spectrum. The war pensions was advised, and my war pension was increased from 20 to 50 per cent, a substantial increase.

However, although I felt better for at least a while, anyway, the nightmares crept in again, the flashbacks too, but this time it wasn't only my problems from the army that were forming the dreams. My childhood was part of it too, the days of hunger, violence, and razor gangs all mixed in with memories of Northern Ireland and the Gulf. I was still drinking and drove the car whilst drunk. I got stopped by the police and was banned from driving, lost my job as a care worker looking after people that were much worse than I was. I loved that job, as I loved the people who I had the privilege to be trusted to take care of.

Now I was left to my own devices and on my own in the house all day whilst Barbara was at work and the boys were at school. Although I didn't drink, it was a terrible existence as I had no one to talk to about how I was feeling. My family was back in Scotland, and Barbara had distanced herself from me. The kids were wondering what was wrong, as they could sense things weren't right, just as I had done when I was a kid. I was history repeating itself and I was becoming my mother. I had PTSD and I am sure my mother had it too, but back then no one knew what that was, just as I didn't on my diagnosis. I was losing control and had lost my marriage, so the drinking became harder and it was every day. I was continually getting arrested by the police for fighting in Blackpool, just picking on anyone, usually doormen who manned the doors to the clubs and pubs. I knew they would give me a good kicking and hoped they would kill me, as the pain inside my head was so great that I didn't want to live. I was taken to hospital on many occasions to be stitched up and then released.

Until the night I will never forget or forgive myself for. I was drinking alone as usual and Barbara was upstairs with the boys watching TV. I asked her if she would like a drink and of course she refused, so I continued to drink and had this thought of going to the garage and getting petrol, but the only thing available was white spirit.

So I filled two plastic juice bottles and said, "That's it, I've had enough, this is the end of the road for me." A war was raging inside my head, and I was losing the battle.

I phoned the police and told them that I made two petrol bombs and that I was holding my wife and children hostage. I had already thrown a petrol bomb onto the road and still had one in my hand.

When the police turned up, they asked me to let Barbara and the children go, which I did immediately, as I was never holding them against their will to start with. I had said this to the police to get urgency; however, I can't even begin to imagine the fear that Barbara must have felt, and that fear transcends from mother to child, just as the fear that I felt from my mother as a child.

I continued to speak to the police negotiator. He asked me what my intention was, and I told him I was going to kill myself. I stood at my front door holding the petrol bomb in my right hand and I lit the taper. There was a skip on my driveway, and I was holding the petrol bomb and threw it underarm into the skip. That was it, game over, and I was arrested by four cops and handcuffed and was on my knees in the front garden.

I was taken to the police station in Lancashire, charged, and locked in a cell. The next morning my solicitor arrived for my interview with CID and I wasn't a well man, that much I knew. How unwell would come out in the psychiatric reports later on. I was initially charged with making an explosive device with the intentions to maim, burn, and kill a police officer.

The negotiator said I looked at him straight in the eye with pure hatred as I threw the petrol bomb directly at him, and that he feared for his life as I intended to burn, mutilate, and disfigure him. But he had said when asked did I aim the petrol at him, as he was standing at the other end of the skip, he said, "Burton threw the petrol bomb underarm and it landed in the skip." If someone is trying to burn you with a petrol bomb and intends to hit you with it, he wouldn't throw it underarm.

My side of the story was recorded and all the evidence was immediately sent to the CPS (crown prosecution service). The intentions to harm anyone was dropped, and a new charge was brought against me of making an explosive device. I read in the local paper many months later that four cops were given police commendations for bravery. I had seen more action in the NAAFI queue. I lay on remand in prison for a year and spent the first six weeks in a cell without a TV or kettle and no money to buy cigarettes. I had no visitors for eighteen months, and in between that I was appearing at court on an average of every two months. All sorts of psychiatric reports were done (six in total), two from the defence, two from the prosecution, and two forensic reports ordered by the judge. All came back with very much the same findings, that I had severe combat PTSD and severe depression.

I was bailed on my first Christmas to a place in North Wales that deals only with veterans with the severest of the condition, and it was run by a great psychiatrist. However, I was only guaranteed two weeks, as it had been funded and paid for by the army benevolent fund. I was improving by the day, as I was with other veterans.

But my time there was short-lived, and back to court I went. This time I was further bailed to an NHS Mental Health Secure Hospital. It was worse than prison. I was surrounded by really sick people who couldn't string a sentence together to have a conversation with. The food was like baby food, all mashed up. I wasn't allowed to carry a lighter, so if I wanted to light my cigarette, I had to ask a member of staff. If they were busy, then you didn't get a light, and it was soul destroying.

It was six weeks of pure hell, but at least Barbara came to see me with the boys, and it was difficult and ripped the heart out of me. My oldest son also came to see me, but he was getting ready to deploy to Iraq and wanted advice from me. It was difficult as during all visits you had a nurse sitting between you so that nothing could be passed over.

But he found it hard and so did I. I waved him goodbye as he walked down the corridor.

I said to myself, "That might be the last time I will see my son," as he was going off to war, just as I'd had to say goodbye to him when I was going to the Gulf War in 1991. I couldn't get to see the news to find out what was going on in Iraq, because all the patients only wanted to watch adverts and the cartoon channel. If you wanted to watch a certain programme, it was put to the vote. I was always outvoted. I felt like Jack Nicholson in *One Flew over the Cuckoo's Nest*. I couldn't wait to get out of this place.

I went back to court yet again, and this time I was remanded back to prison, as the psychiatrist said that being in the secure hospital was doing more harm than good. I never thought that I would look forward to going back to prison, but a least I could talk to people there. My son was in Iraq and I was in a prison cell, but at least now I had a TV and could keep up-to-date with what was happening over there.

That year rolled by, and my son had made it back home safe. So many hadn't come back, but I was still on remand, still not sentenced. The judge wanted a hospital order for me instead of a prison sentence. After thirteen separate appearances at court over a year on remand and him fighting with the PCT (primary care trust), they refused to fund me to go to hospital.

At that, the judge said to her, "Do you think it's fair that I send a man

It Cuts Me Deeply

to prison who served his country and of the consequence of that service has suffered? If you don't fund him, then I have no choice."

She said, "We can't."

The judge dismissed her, and at that he turned to me and said, "Burton, stand up."

I stood there bolt upright, and he said to me, "It is with regret that I send you to prison today for five and a half years, with a recommendation to the Home Secretary that you are transferred to a hospital as soon as possible for the treatment that you so richly deserve. Take him down."

I was off, and at least now I had a release date. My barrister came to see me in the holding cells below the court and told me we were going to appeal the length of my sentence. It took another year for that to come through.

My second Christmas in prison, and my mind went back to my childhood of Christmases going hungry or going to the Salvation Army for presents, and all the times that I had been in Northern Ireland over the Christmas period and the fact that it was the time of year that my two friends had been killed by the IRA. I was missing my boys, hadn't seen them for about a year. It was a crushing time for me, but you can't show weakness in prison or you won't last long. Just two months before I'd tried to throw this big guy over the rail of the top landing, as he kept moaning about getting eighteen month for killing a guy in Blackpool. He'd been working as a doorman and pushed this junkie over. The junkie hit his head on the pavement and died two or three days later.

After that I was put in a cell on my own, as I was now classed as high risk. That suited me as I could watch what I wanted on the TV and could keep my cell clean and tidy, but I took shit from no one. I got a job as a cleaner on the landing, as the prison officer that was in charge was ex-Royal Marines, and as soon as he read my file and saw that I'd been a soldier, he asked me if I took drugs and I said, "No, Boss." So he offered me the job. He was a brilliant guy and looked after me.

There were two other cleaners that I worked alongside. One was called James, who was doing sixteen years for killing his father in-law, who had abused James's wife when she was a child, and the other was Joe, who cut a guy with a chain saw many years previously but was now doing nine years for stabbing his boyfriend multiple times and watched him die on the floor.

His boyfriend was trying to crawl to the phone, but Joe kept kicking it away, eventually letting him call an ambulance. I asked Joe why he stabbed him, and he said he'd been cheating on him with a woman.

He said, "I wouldn't have minded if it had been another guy, but a whore bitch? He was two-timing me with a woman."

Joe and I got on well, but I was always on my guard with him as he could turn in a moment. He was a little skinny guy, and I could have snapped his neck in a second, but he would do a lot of damage to you if he got a chance.

We would hang over the landing and watch the new prisoners coming in, and if he saw someone that he fancied, he would say, "Bomber, do you think he's nice?"

I'd say, "Joe, I'm not gay," and he would say, "I know, but you're educated, and if you say he's nice, then he must be nice."

I'd say, "He's OK."

That was enough for Joe, and he'd be on him right away. If the guy happened to be gay also, he would be in Joe's cell that night during association. They were all young guys.

I said, "Why haven't you tried it on with me?"

He would say, "I like them young, Bomber."

And I said, "Thank God."

I used to write letters for him since he couldn't read or write, which took me straight back to when I tried to join the army but couldn't read or write. So I was giving something back for the education that had been afforded me. He used to ask me to educate him, and I would spend hours telling him all the history of the Nazis and the Second World War, and he wanted to know about my time in Northern Ireland.

But you had to be careful with that one, as Joe had ancestors from Ireland, like most of us, but he took it personally, and if he disagreed with something, you had to either agree or persuade him that what you were saying was fact. We used to watch Trooping the Colour in my cell, but you had to ask the prison staff for permission. He would plead with them to let him watch with me, as he told them that Bomber was going to tell him all about the different guards on parade. So for peace sake they would allow him and he loved it. I used to write letters to his son for him.

It Cuts Me Deeply

Joe was bisexual, and he was a damaged man and had been in and out of prison all his life.

My release date came and I had won my appeal at the Royal Courts of Justice in London, and my sentence was reduced to three and a half years. By the time it had come through I only had ten days of my sentence left to do. However, I wasn't free, as the Home Office had decided that I was to be transferred to a psychiatric hospital – and it was to be funded by the same PCT that had refused to fund me two years and eight months earlier. I was leaving prison, and that was great news, even though I was going to another institution for God only knows how long. As I was under a Home Office transfer and was under a section order, it could be many years. I had prepared myself psychologically for this. It was tough saying goodbye to Joe. I wouldn't have stood on the same side of the street of him on the outside, but in prison you have to make the best of a bad lot.

On the day of my transfer, the cell door opened and it wasn't the prison officers that I knew. These guys were different. This was the nutting squad that dealt with prisoners that were to be nutted off, and I was one of them. My hair hadn't been cut in two years, my beard was down to my chest, and I had lost about two stone in weight.

They put double handcuffs on me and a belt around my waist, two officers on either side of me, and I boarded a transit van with bars on the windows and four prison officers with me.

We arrived at this well-known, swanky hospital, and they took me in as all the other clients are looking at me and I dare say were shitting themselves as this thing full of hair with a Glaswegian accent had landed on their door.

The psychiatrist turned up, and the first thing he said to them was to remove the cuffs, and they said, "Once you've signed for him."

He signed and the cuffs were removed. My first day at the hospital had begun, and hopefully they could put me back together. I didn't hold out too much hope; too much damage had been done over too many years.

I was taken to my room and very nice it was; it had a TV and telephone with en suite shower and bathroom. Most of the clients there had either drug or alcohol problems – throw in a bit of depression too. They were paying for their treatment themselves, either through their private medical insurance or their rich parents, and it wasn't cheap. If I remember it was something like £540 per week. It was a private hospital after all, the place where all the stars and celebrities go, and here I was a prison transfer and the bill getting picked up by the Home Office. As you can imagine there were a couple of resentments flying around, but they didn't know my story yet.

Barbara came to visit. She hadn't seen me since I was in Victoria Psychiatric Hospital two years earlier. She was shown to my room and the door was opened. She burst out crying and couldn't believe I was the same man that she had married.

I sat on the edge of the bed. I had lost so much weight, and the length of my hair and beard frightened her and the boys. The boys were scared to come near me at first, but as soon as I spoke they realised who I was, and we cuddled each other and started on the long road of getting to know one another again. You have to remember I had carried out an act that had traumatised them, and I knew it and hated myself, as I loved them so much.

They left after about an hour, which seemed to just disappear in no time at all. I asked Barbara if she would visit me again and she said that she would. "Great," I said.

After they all left, I was further assessed by the psychiatrist, and a care package was formulated for my duration. There was no need for detox as I had been dry for more than two years. It was strange walking about this lavish place, given what I had just come from.

At first the other patients were a bit reluctant to come near me. They knew I had just come from prison and thought I might be dangerous, which I wasn't. In fact, I was more scared than they were. Again I judged myself, thinking I didn't deserve to be here in such a beautiful place and getting this treatment from the finest in the country – or so I thought. I received one-to-one counselling for my PTSD and it wasn't the best, I must admit, as I felt they didn't understand combat-related trauma and instead kept focussing on the alcohol addiction and group therapy. It was difficult for me to open up in front of these people who had depression and anxiety and came from middle- and upper-class backgrounds, who were drinking a little too much red wine at night after a hard day at the office. How could I sit there and tell them my story? It would have traumatised them even more just listening to me.

Barbara came up the next day, but this time she brought scissors and cut my hair. She brought my shaving kit from the house and pyjamas, and when I took off my top, she cried again as she could see all my ribs and bone structure of my shoulders. My muscle group had deteriorated so much and my legs were like pins. I had lost just under two stone and hadn't been out in the fresh air for most of my time in prison. It would take time and I knew it.

The therapy continued, and I became even more distant from the group therapy, as I was listening to the shit that these people were saying and why they were depressed. This one woman was depressed because she had horses and one of them wouldn't foal. I felt like throwing her out the window, but I suppose it was a big deal to her in her middle-class lifestyle.

On Saturday mornings the AA attendees would come to the hospital, and we'd have a two-hour meeting and then lunch. After that the patients were allowed out with their families for four hours of shopping, although none of them were being kept there against their will, as they were informal patients and could have left at any time. But the agreement was a six-week residency. I wasn't allowed out as I was on a Home Office Section Order, for at least now. I could have run away at any time, as there was no barbed wire fences or security guards, but I didn't have anywhere to go, and I would have been caught and probably sent to a high security mental hospital where they hold serial killers. That's where the judge wanted to send me had the PCT agreed at court to fund a hospital order. Looking back, it turned out better that I was sent to prison rather than end up in a place like that.

Eventually I came off the section and was allowed out just like the rest of them. Barbara used to come up on a Saturday with the kids, and we would go out and do a bit of shopping and a bit of lunch. It was good to see the outside again and to have fun with the boys, albeit if only for a few hours and then back to the hospital. My legs were very weak, and I couldn't walk a great distance, too much muscle wastage, so I decided to buy a push bike as I was determined to get myself fit again. The nearest town was Kirkham about eight kilometres away, so I planned one Saturday morning to cycle there and back. Sixteen kilometres, not a problem, as back in the day it would just have been a warm-up for me.

But now was different. I was shocked at how weak I had become. I could hardly push the peddles down, but day by day I got stronger. The food was top-notch, and they gave us as much fruit as we could eat. I wasn't drinking and was getting good quality sleep. At the beginning I was on 250mg of all sorts of medication from the prison – the "liquid cosh" we called it – to keep you docile. The hospital took me off all this.

Before I knew it I was cycling there and back to Kirkham, with no problems. Part of my treatment plan was a gym membership, and I started going. A car was sent to pick us up, along with a gym instructor, all paid for by the priory, or in my case the Home Office. The guys in the regiment visited, and it was great to see them all. We had some laughs and it really cheered me up.

Barbara came to see me on this particular Saturday, and I could tell by the look on her face that something was wrong. She cried and went into her handbag and handed me an envelope. Inside was a letter stating that she had started divorce proceedings. I was gutted, but I understood. How could she ever trust me again after what I had done?

Now I was truly on my own, although to be honest she did keep visiting me throughout my time in the hospital, and so did the guys from the regiment. One of my mates was visiting me this one particular Saturday morning, and all of a sudden this cleaner ran past us crying. We asked her what was wrong and she said there had been a terrible accident outside. So I and my pal ran out to see what was wrong.

This guy was lying on his back. He had fallen off his motorbike after hitting an oncoming car. As I looked at him I knew he was dead. His eyes were open, but the glaze had come over them. I call it the dead man's stare, and I had seen it many times before. The one that gets me is the UDR soldier, when he had been shot in Omagh. Although half his face was missing, he had one remaining eye that was wide open with the same glaze over it. So I knew this guy was dead, but we still tried to give CPR as only a doctor can pronounce someone dead. As my pal pressed down his chest, all this black gunge came out of his mouth.

The police arrived along with an air ambulance with a doctor, and he pronounced him dead, so the helicopter disappeared and the mortuary van turned up and took him away. All the staff from the hospital were watching this unfold, and I was the patient working on a casualty along with my mate from the regiment. Two days later the police came to take a statement from me, and the hospital staff were shitting themselves in case I held them responsible for my being exposed to this extra trauma whilst under their care. I don't work that way, and besides, it didn't even cross my mind.

I spent six months in the hospital at a cost to the taxpayers of £74.000, where had they listened to Dr George Benson, who specialised in combat PTSD. It would have cost no more than the NHS of £9.000, refused by the same PCT who shelved out all this money to this swanky money-making hospital.

I was due for release, but I was homeless and had nowhere to go, with still unattended deep underlying psychological issues that hadn't been addressed by the swanky money-making racket of a private cabal.

I eventually found a place on the north shore of Blackpool, and what a state this place was in. It was riddled with dampness, and the rain was coming in through the side of the window. What more could I expect as the rent was only £150 per month? I began to withdraw into myself again as I had gone the full circle of poverty. I had started off life in poverty and now I was back at the beginning, but this time much older and alone with a headful of demons and a drink problem, a situation that was exacerbating. I had all sorts of arseholes coming and going at night to the flats above, and a drugs den I kept well clear of, and I just tried to remain focussed.

But it was getting harder by the day. Barbara would come and see me with the boys, and at this time I got my war pension back as it had been stopped from the day I got sentenced until I came out of hospital. I got back quite a lot of money, plus benefits that I was entitled to, that the Royal British Legion had sorted out for me. I think I got back about £3,500 of which I gave a big chunk to Barbara for the boys, as my 12-year-old was starting big school so he needed all sorts of kit for that.

But apart from it being my duty to do this, it was my boys and wife who needed this money and not me, as it was me that had messed things up and not them. I continued to drink everyday watching the world go by and my health was deteriorating by the day. I started to lose weight again, mainly through stress and not eating. I had no heating in the flat, the TV didn't work properly as there was no outside aerial, and I slept in my army sleeping bag. To think this bag had been in the desert and on the fields of South Armagh ... now it was still looking after me in a rundown flat in

Blackpool's north shore amongst the dropouts and people on the fringes of life, whom no one cared about anymore.

I made the decision, for which I will always regret, to move to Clacton, Essex, after my friend said, "Why don't you move down beside me? It's got to be better than this."

Yes, it was better than what I was living in at the time.

He said, "You'll be closer to your oldest son."

I made the decision to move, so I called my pal to see if he would do my move and he said yes. We loaded up and off we went, but I felt totally crushed. My heart was aching and dying inside, and all the way down I kept thinking, "How selfish could I be to be leaving my sons behind?" It still hurts me to this day, and I hate myself for that selfish act. I love my boys, but I never gave it a thought to think how this would affect them and what they must be feeling, just like when I was a kid and wanted to be with my dad.

I moved into a flat in Clacton, of which my pal and his partner had paid the deposit and first month's rent, and I would pay them back once I was sorted out. I wasn't there long as the girl down below complained to the landlord that I was drinking every night and talking too loudly. The soundproofing wasn't that great, and I tend to speak loudly when drinking as I am deaf in one ear due to mortar fire, but she continued to complain.

One morning she came to my door screaming in my face, and I had just woken up out of a drunken sleep and she was banging on my door, so I told her to piss off. But she kept screaming at me, so I shoved her away and slapped her across the face.

The cops arrived and I was arrested and taken back to court as I was still out on license from prison, which meant I could be recalled to serve the rest of my sentence of two years.

I went to court, and this girl said that I had punched her, and the judge asked the police if she had been injured or had any marks on her and the police said no. I was found guilty and given six months in prison, deferred for two years, the time that I had left on my licence. I had to attend probation for the next two years. You see, alcohol was my Achilles heel and it was destroying me, just as it had my mother. Throw in all the other damage and one feeds off the other, and life becomes so chaotic and

It Cuts Me Deeply

unmanageable, you drink to ease the pain, but the alcohol brings more pain and then you drink on that pain and so the vicious cycle continues.

They say the definition of madness is to continue with the same behaviour and expect a different outcome.

I moved in to a flat in Clacton. This time it was owned by my pal, and only he could kick me out. The flat was lovely, and you could play your music as loud as you wanted as it was right in the centre of town. The only problem was that all the drunks were pissing on my door. It drove me crazy, I came out my door one morning and someone had done a shite on my doorstep. I came from the pub one night and these two guys are pissing on my door, so I grabbed one of them and pushed him away. I walked inside my flat, and within seconds my door was getting smashed down. These three guys came inside. I tried to throw a punch at one of them, but I was hit on the side of my head with one of my table lamps and then another, and after that I was hit with all sorts of stuff, punched, kicked, and stomped on and left in a heap on the floor.

Blood poured from everywhere: my mouth, nose, and head. I called my pal, but he was asleep drunk. Jane came down and was the state I was in and called an ambulance. The paramedics gave me six staples to the back of my head and I was taken to Colchester General for an X-ray of my arm. I had a broken elbow and it was put in plaster.

My pal came down the next day, and we went round every pub in Clacton looking for them, but we couldn't find them. It could have been so much worse if they had been carrying knives.

I went on dating sites and had a great time. I went on quite a few dates, until I met a woman by the name of Liz. We hit it off instantly; she had everything I was looking for in a woman: she was pretty and elegant with a beautiful voice and the sexiest wiggle I had ever seen, and my heart missed a beat every time I looked at her. The sex was amazing and electric. I fell head-over-heels in love with her and would have cut my heart out for her. But I felt beneath her and not good enough, as I didn't have a job, and I wasn't long out of hospital after two and a half years in prison. This reinforced my insecurities of never being introduced to her friends or being included in any photos on her Facebook page. It was like I didn't exist; I was the invisible boyfriend.

We argued quite a bit over silly things, and she would walk out and it would be over for a couple of weeks, and then we would be back together again until the next argument. But the thing that wore me down the most and broke my heart was that she would tell me that she had been dating other guys, and at least they were comfortable in their own skin and not a quivering wreck like me. All this ate into my heart and took me straight back to my childhood and the way my mother used to put me down all my life.

I would ask myself, "What am I doing wrong? How can I win this woman's respect?" All I ever wanted was to meet a woman and love her with all I had to offer. I have never cheated on anyone in all my life. When I'm in a relationship, it's honest.

We continued to see each other over the next two years and ten months until it finally came to an end on Easter weekend 2011. We were at Pizza Express or something of that nature and had an argument over the price and I stormed out, with Liz in hot pursuit. We were arguing in the street. We got into my car, and my son is in the backseat. We're still arguing all the way to her house, and she told me to collect my things and get out.

I left and knew it was over. When I went home to my flat a couple of weeks later, my boots were at the front entrance. She had dropped them off. I never saw her again. But I never stopped loving her.

I went on a couple of dates after that, but Liz had destroyed something inside me. I don't think I've ever loved anyone more than her. I don't know, maybe if she had met me before my illness had taken hold of me, when I was confident and strong of body and mind, things might have been different. It's all maybes. We will never know.

I moved back to Glasgow in 2013 and was sofa surfing for a few months as I was homeless. It broke my heart as I had to give my little dog, Rosie, away as I couldn't have her suffer. Two women in my life that I often think of are Liz and wee Rosie.

Eventually the council got me a flat in a tenement in Glasgow. Now I had come full circle back to my roots where I was born. It wasn't the place I remembered; it had changed so much. It had been taken over by the living dead, junkies and real lowlifes.

One Saturday afternoon I was watching TV. It was a hot summer day, and I heard marching band music. I looked out the window and saw the Irish Tri-Colour. They're all wearing black berets and dark sunglasses. It was a Republican Irish flute band. I had an instant panic attack as I was immediately back in Crossmaglen in Northern Ireland. I had to get out of this place.

I went into a pub at Glasgow Cross in the city centre wearing my veterans badge. I walked up to the bar to order a pint, and the Irish Tri-Colour and Celtic photos are on the wall. These people would kick me to death if they had seen that badge. Being away from Glasgow for so long, I had forgotten that this place is very dangerous for ex-soldiers, if you happen to be in the wrong place at the wrong time.

One day I and my brother James went to see a Celtic play, and all the good old Celtic songs were being sung, and it was a great atmosphere.

But all of a sudden the mood changed and they sang IRA songs.

I looked at my brother and said, "I can't listen to this."

He said, "Richard, there's nothing we can do about it. We're here to see the Celtic play, not to listen to the braindead sing their shite."

I have never been back.

My family was getting to know me all over again, as they hadn't seen me since 2000 and since my diagnoses of PTSD. They hadn't visited me in prison, so I wasn't the same guy, and I could sense that they felt that, and it crushed me too. I was a stranger. They had moved on with their lives whilst mine was stuck in the past. I was still in Northern Ireland or the Iraqi desert.

I don't want or expect pity; all I want is to be me again. Maybe that will never happen, but I get by with my writing about the troubles of Northern Ireland, it helps me process the things I have seen and done. Most people come back from conflicts unscathed. I'm just one of the unfortunate ones that was affected. When at Combat Stress, I asked the nurse, "Why did I get PTSD and others didn't?"

Her answer was, "It happened to you, Richard, because you cared."

But there isn't a hole deep enough that I won't climb out of. Now I had become a recluse and didn't go out much. I wasn't the same person they remembered of being confident and the life and soul of the party. A lot of water has gone under the bridge, along with a lot of tears and pain.

I was talking to a guy called Blue Lagoon that I had served with and hadn't seen since I got out of the regiment. Now I was back in Scotland, and he invited me up to his home in Crieff, just outside Perth. He picked me up at the bus station, and I couldn't believe he was living in a beautiful cottage.

I said, "Blue, how much did this cost you?"

He said, "I don't own it, it's a veterans house."

I said, "How did you go about getting one of these?"

He told me that he just applied for it through an organisation called Scottish Veterans Garden City, so I got back to Glasgow on the Monday and went to a place called Helping Heroes and asked them if they knew anything about veterans housing.

The lady said yes and invited me into her office. She went on the computer and up came a list of house. They were all over Scotland, so I applied for the area that I wanted and waited. After about a month I got a letter to go to Charing Cross, the same place that I had gone to in the early 1970s with my dad to the Salvation Army to get Christmas presents.

I went in and I was told that I would have to be interviewed by a board, and if successful I would then have to get a final interview. I did the interview and was told I would get a letter in due course as to whether I had been successful.

About six weeks later got a phone call from a retired major. He said, "I hear you have applied for a veteran's house. Well, you've been successful. Don't worry, you have one final interview. Glad to have you back with us."

I got the keys on 20 June 2015, and I couldn't have been happier. I've got great neighbours in a quiet area, the upmarket side of Paisley, a street of forty veterans – my own kind of people, people with honour and decency. I hope now that this will be my final rendezvous.

I still don't go out much, still have the same demons, except no one sees them anymore. I hide away, getting the occasional visit from my nephew and his partner. If I'm honest they are the only ones who visit me. I do occasionally visit my brother James and his wife, or my sister Annette, but if truth be told if I didn't visit them, I wouldn't see anyone. I can sit for three months without a visit from anyone, and every day is groundhog day.

They say the biggest prison to be in is in your own mind.

I would love to meet someone again, but time is marching on and I am now 60 years old. I have been on my own now since I broke up with Liz in 2011, only going on a couple of dates, but although the women I dated were nice and attractive too, I just felt like I didn't belong with anyone, anymore. I am at the end of the road now, and no more tarmac is getting laid ahead for me.

I don't know how long I have left in this world as all my pals from the regiment are dropping like flies. I can tell you it's not been a good journey, and if I could have had any input into my being born, I would have opted out.

Where do I go from here? Well, I sit alone every day and reflect on my life throughout the decades – the mistakes and misjudgements and stupidity of what could have been a promising army career and a happy marriage, with all my sons around me as they grew into men and the usual Sunday visit of grandchildren and the cosy Christmases of what others take for granted.

It wasn't to be, at least not for me. As I watch the kids coming home from school and walking with their mothers and how happy they all are, I have to turn away as I can feel the tears welling up in my eyes. No one knows as I walk along the street of how lonely and empty my life is. I have made my bed and now must lie in it; it's the way it is because of my behaviour and the demons that have plagued me all my life and still do, except there is no one here to see my pain and the tears that I shed throughout a day and the difficulty I have trying to get through what has become nothing more than a twenty-four-hour clock. They say you reap what you sow. Well, this is my damnation for all my ills. I try to show kindness now to everyone I meet, and like my dad, I don't like discord or confrontations. Those days are over.

Violence solves nothing but only begets violence, with not only the original problem still unresolved but another problem created. Oh how I wished I had taken this advice forty years ago, but in the words of the great playwright George Bernard Shaw, "Youth is wasted on the young." I only have memories left now, and I don't suppose I will be making any new ones. I am in pain every day of my life, with arthritis and my bowels not working properly. I struggle with anxiety and depression, and my life has become insular and very much in isolation most of the time. I speak to the neighbours but only in passing, really only to say hello and see you later. I have spent the last five Christmases on my own – not that I haven't had invites from family and friends, but as I have said, I find Christmas a very sad time. I find it difficult to look forward to anything or enjoy it anymore.

As I write this final chapter of my life story as best I can, you must remember that I am not a trained writer or a writer of any description, but I have tried my best, purely from memory, to convey to you all how my life was and is.

I hope I haven't offended anyone or embellished the truth. That was not my intention.

Lightning Source UK Ltd.
Milton Keynes UK
UKHW010226280520
363924UK00001BA/105